Garlic & Olive Oil

Bringing family together with food

By
Emily I. Vannoni

www.garlicandoliveoil.com

www.garlicandoliveoil.com

For my sister, Angie

www.garlicandoliveoil.com

Table of Contents

Introduction

Oh where to begin… To me food is EVERYTHING. So many of my memories revolve around food in one way or another. There are the obvious ones like:

Christmas Eve = ham and clam chowder
Christmas = beef tenderloin
Birthdays = whatever I want that year
Weddings = I'm only there to judge your cake

But it goes beyond that. To me, childhood weekends were sitting at the kitchen table while I "help" my Grandma Inchiostro make meatballs and sauce; eating watermelon on Uncle Doc's porch. Monday night football was Dad's fried oysters, buttered toast, oranges and a little champagne if we were extra lucky. Junior high summers were spent in front of the TV with my sister and brother, in our sleeping bags watching Julia Child (and Bob Ross). When Dad got home it was Yan Can Cook (and Dr. Who). High school is popping over to Aunt May's house to swim at her pool while eating stuffed artichokes and Amighetti sandwiches. And so on and so forth until we come to adulthood where all vacations are planned around restaurants.

I come from a big Italian family. For those of you who do also, I assume you already understand what I am talking about. For the rest of you, I will do my best to explain. I think most would agree that three of the most important things in this world are life, love and family. Food is what brings them all together. We celebrate with food and it celebrates our history. It is really like a family tree and an old photo album all rolled into one. It is the one thing that can immediately bring you back to some special moment in time. You may think I am going too far but I am just trying to explain why I believe food is everything. And subsequently why I actually get offended when people do not appreciate it. But I will table that for now.

In this book you will find a collection of recipes. I did not create all of them but I will try to hand out all credit where it is due. I'm sure that will just be a jumping off point for everyone in the family. I can already hear the, "You know, I'm really the one that came up with that recipe." Or, "that's not how Grandma did it." And, "Why didn't you put this in there, you know I make it really good." I look forward to next Christmas already!

So, I hope you will use this cookbook as a tool. Make something you are proud of, share it with your friends and family. Sit down around the table; leave the phones and TV off. Talk to each other; make new memories and create your own family traditions.

The Players

This whole cookbook grew out of a plan to gather family recipes for my sister. Without the contributions of my family it never would have happened. I thank them for their recipes, time, energy, motivation and unwavering support. Although many people have made this possible a special shout out to my grandparents, parents and aunts without whom this book would not exist. They have each included (at least) one recipe and I always think it's nice to be able to put a face with a name. So, let's meet them:

Grandma & Grandpa Inchiostro

Grandpa & Grandma Babor

Mom, Me & Dad

The Inchiostros: Dad, Aunt Carol, Aunt Clare & Aunt May

The Babors: Aunt Julie, Aunt Kathleen, Aunt Marjorie, Aunt Joy, Mom & Aunt Sheryl

Understanding This Cookbook

To make the most out of this cookbook you will need to understand a little bit about how these recipes were collected, how I cook as well as what my tastes are. This will make you more successful in tailoring recipes to suit you and your family. I always would advise you to follow the recipe the first time and then change it up, if you feel like it, after that initial try.

That being said, let's look at the potential shortcomings of this book…

First of all, most recipes were either verbally told to me or I made them with the person who passed them down to me. A lot of these people measure NOTHING!!! I was literally yelled at several times when asked, "How much?" The responses were something like "when it smells right" or "if you want a lot put a lot in, if you want a little use a little." Very helpful. As a result, some things took me a few tries before they tasted like I remembered they should. I tried to get the measurements right but I just thought I should let you know that up front.

Also, I love garlic! I usually put at least double of whatever is called for in a recipe. If garlic is not your favorite then you might not want to put in as much as I recommend. But really… you should (again, at least the first time). It will taste better.

Most all salt and pepper will be done to taste. I will try to put in initial measurements where I can but really, this is up to you. And when I say salt, I am always talking about kosher salt. If I mean another type I will let you know. I am also always talking about fresh ground black pepper when I say pepper. Oh, and always use Garlic Powder (the granulated garlic, not actual powder), never Garlic Salt.

Olive Oil always means Extra-Virgin Olive Oil. If I mean something else, I will let you know.

Butter is always unsalted butter.

When I say Parmesan cheese I always mean Parmigiano-Reggiano imported from Italy.

Almost all herbs are fresh herbs. The only dried herbs I use are Bay Leaves, Herbes de Provence and Italian Seasoning. If I don't mean fresh I will say "dried." Everything else you should snip from your garden or pick up in the fresh herb section of the grocery store. And, I always use flat leaf Italian parsley, not curly parsley. You can use whatever you like but all measurements are based on flat leaf parsley.

I keep a piece of foil on the bottom rack of my oven. This keeps the bottom of my oven clean. I imagine it also changes cooking times slightly so I thought I should let you know. But I've never had a grease fire.

I also have a gas grill. Everything will of course work on a charcoal grill and probably taste better. But instructions will be written for a gas grill because I am impatient and hungry.

I like food that is simple and delicious. A beginner can make almost all of these recipes. That is not to say there aren't some time consuming recipes but most things are pretty easy. And most ingredients are very common. I'm not a fan of buying an ingredient that I will only use in one dish. Seems like a waste of money to me.

My instructions are rather verbose. I don't want you to be intimidated if you see a "long" recipe. I tried to be very specific when explaining the preparations to give you the best chance of making a successful dish.

Abbreviations:

oz = ounce
tsp = teaspoon
T = tablespoon
c = cup
lb/lbs = pound/pounds
pkg = package

My whole goal is to make people love creating an entire experience. In the back of the book there are menu plans for different occasions, from a backyard barbecue to a romantic dinner, to help you on your journey.

Go forth and conquer!

Top Ten Tips

1. Olive oil, salt and pepper is all you need for most things to taste their most delicious. Meat, vegetables, bread, you name it. These three ingredients will get you very far.

2. Whenever a recipe says "stew meat" use short ribs. You will thank me.

3. When grilling meat, flip one time. Same goes for "browning" or "searing" meat. Put it on and don't touch it.

4. When adding garlic to a recipe, only let it cook for about 30 seconds, stirring constantly until you add a liquid. It burns quickly and you have to wash the pan before that taste goes away.

5. Don't make things harder than they need to be. If you can't make it better than something you can buy in the store, then buy it in the store. For example, I do not make my own baguettes. I don't have the time or patience for that.

6. Soak all berries in a mixture of 1 part plain distilled vinegar to 9 parts water. Just drop them in and give them a little swirl with your hand. After about a minute take them out and let them dry on a cookie sheet lined with paper towels (no need to rinse again). Then, store them back in their original container lined with a dry paper towel. Do this as soon as you get them home from the store. Not only will this make your berries last twice as long but look at all the dirt in the bottom of the bowl when you dump out the water. Aren't you glad you aren't eating that!

7. There are some ingredients that just make everything better or are so versatile you might always want to have them laying around. Two that spring to mind are truffle butter and Wishbone Italian Dressing. These are used for very different things but they make something ordinary turn into the extraordinary.

> Use truffle butter (which you should buy on sale and then keep in the freezer) to fry your eggs, put a dollop on your burger or steak, add it to pasta or veggies, swirl a little in your gravy.
>
> Use Wishbone Italian Dressing to make boring chicken breasts or bland pork chops amazingly flavorful. Chop some tomatoes and avocados, throw them in a bowl and squeeze on some dressing; simple, fast and absolutely delicious!

8. When cooking pasta and sauce there are several key things to know:

After the water has started to boil, HEAVILY salt the water before putting in your noodles. This is your chance to flavor the pasta itself.

If finishing the pasta in a sauce, cook it 1 minute less than the "al dente" recommendation. The noodles will continue to cook in the sauce and you don't want them to be mushy.

Using tongs or a spider, move pasta directly from the boiling water to the pot of sauce. Do not drain the noodles then add to the sauce. This way if you need to thin the sauce or bring it together, you can use the pasta water to do so. If you absolutely have to drain the pasta for some reason, always save at least a cup of the pasta water before draining.

The best way to mix/toss/serve pasta is with tongs. I don't even know why they make those spaghetti spoons. They are terrible.

9. When preparing anything that cooks for hours: pasta sauces, soups, stews, short ribs, etc. always add a handful of fresh herbs at the very end and for garnish when serving. It will brighten up a slow simmering dish.

10. Make a batch of breadcrumbs (pg. 108) now and put them in your freezer. You will have a head start on so many recipes in this book.

Breakfast

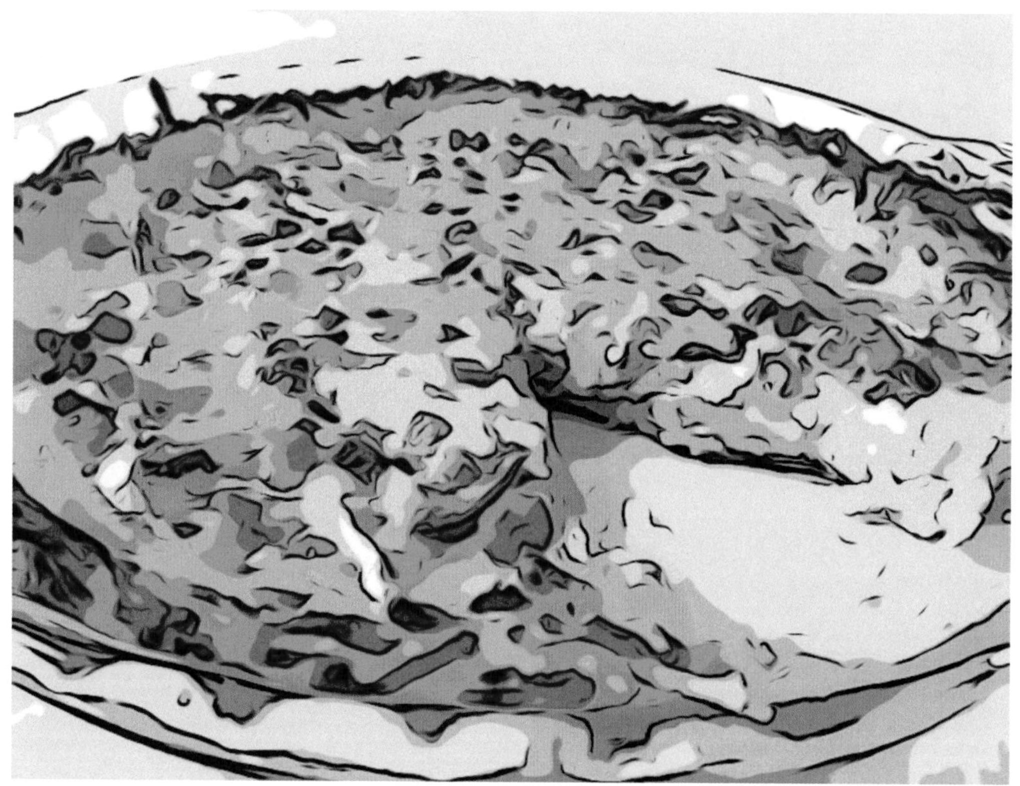

Ham & Brie Breakfast Bake

Breakfast & Brunch

Breakfast Crepes

Egg Casserole

Egg Salad

Granola

Ham & Brie Breakfast Bake

Orange Fruit Salad

Overnight French Toast

Perfect Boiled Eggs

Quiche

Sausage Gravy

Smoked Salmon Spread

Breakfast Crepes

About 20 Crepes

Aunt Clare

Growing up, we had a lot of sleepovers at Aunt Clare's house. Every time we got to spend the night, all I wanted the next morning for breakfast were Aunt Clare's crepes. If I didn't ask for them every time, I was always hoping for them… always! These are so versatile- eat them plain, like pancakes, fill with jam, fill with fruit (might I recommend chocolate hazelnut spread and banana)… the sky is the limit!

Ingredients:

2 c Milk
4 Eggs
2 c Flour
2 tsp Sugar
1 tsp Salt

Add all ingredients to a blender and blend until well combined; the batter will be thin.

Spoon 3T of batter onto a hot, greased 6-7" skillet, tilting the pan so batter is distributed to edges.
Brown lightly on one side, flip and brown on the other side.
Stack on a warm platter and serve.

Serving Option 2:
Spread a filling of your choice and roll up. Place in a buttered baking dish, sprinkle with powdered sugar and heat in a 300 degree oven for about 5 minutes. Serve topped with sour cream.

Egg Casserole

Serves 12

Aunt Sheryl

I love Easter Brunch! My Aunt Sheryl and Uncle Steve make a delicious Easter Brunch; it might be my favorite meal of the year. Although she always tries to make something a little different each year- it would not be Easter Brunch without this egg casserole (and a ham of course)! It is a delicious breakfast dish for any time of the year but we still think of it as a special occasion in our house. That is how it also wiggled its way to becoming our Christmas morning tradition too.

Ingredients:
2½ c Croutons
2 c Sharp Cheddar
2 lbs Breakfast Sausage (I like Jimmy Dean- Regular)
6 Eggs
¾ tsp Mustard
2½ c Milk, divided
10½ oz can Cream of Mushroom Soup

Layer croutons in greased 9x13 pan.
Layer cheese on top of croutons.
Crumble, brown and drain sausage; layer over cheese.
Beat eggs, mustard and 2 c milk together; pour over sausage.
Cover and refrigerate over night.

The next morning… Preheat oven to 300
Blend ½ c milk and cream of mushroom soup; spoon on top of casserole.
Bake 1½ hours.

Egg Salad

Serves 6-12

What to do with all those eggs you dyed for Easter? What to serve for a tea party? Egg salad of course. I like mine simple, no relish or whatever else people add to take away from the egg flavor. I'm a purist. Serve on soft bread spread with a little mayo and some watercress. Simple and delicious. If you are going true tea party style, cut into triangles or other dainty shapes.

Ingredients:
12 Hard-Boiled Eggs (pg. 21)
½ tsp Salt
¼ tsp Pepper
1/3 c Mayonnaise
2 tsp Whole Grain Mustard*
2 tsp Dijon Mustard*
2 tsp Yellow Mustard*

*If you don't have these just use 2 Tablespoons of your favorite mustard, but the combo does give it a nice flavor and texture.

Chop eggs and put in mixing bowl.
Add remaining ingredients and mix until well blended. Taste for seasoning.

Granola

Makes 3½ - 4 Cups

I have to admit, I am pretty proud of coming up with this recipe. It is quite yummy. My husband eats it like cereal, I love to eat it with yogurt and my sister has found another use- a topping for ice cream... not bad sister! It also makes a great gift for teachers, a hostess, etc.

Ingredients:

2 c Oats
¼ c Sunflower Seeds
½ c Sliced Almonds
¼ c Coconut Flakes
¼ c Brown Sugar
½ tsp Salt
1/8 c Honey
1/8 c Maple Syrup
scant ¼ c Vegetable Oil
2/3 – ¾ c Dried Fruit (just one or a combo)

Preheat oven to 250
Combine the first 6 ingredients together in large bowl.
Mix last 3 ingredients together in a separate bowl or glass measuring cup.
Gradually pour the wet ingredients into the oat mixture while stirring; toss well to make sure everything is evenly coated.
Pour mix into single layer on large sheet pan lined with parchment paper.
Cook 1 hour and 15 minutes stirring every 15 minutes.
Remove from oven and let cool on the sheet pan.

After completely cooled mix in the dried fruit (rec dried cherries, chopped dried apricots are a close second). Store in an airtight container; it will keep for weeks.

Ham & Brie Breakfast Bake

Serves 6-8

This is basically in between an egg casserole and a quiche. It is very yummy and quite versatile. In this recipe I use ham and Brie but you could use any meat and cheese combination you like. My husband prefers it with shredded Colby Jack cheese but I want to use Brie whenever I can because I LOVE IT! Another great thing about this recipe- you can cook the crust the night before and store it covered in the fridge (this really cuts down on the prep time in the morning).

Ingredients:
20 oz pkg of refrigerated (shredded) Hash Browns, at room temperature
1/3 c Butter, melted
1 tsp Salt
1 c diced Ham
4-6 oz Brie, sliced (or 1 c shredded cheese)
2 Eggs
½ c Heavy Whipping Cream

Preheat oven to 425
In a large bowl mix the hash browns, butter and salt.
Press the mixture into the bottom and up the sides of a pie plate *(the potatoes will really shrink while they cook so make sure they go all the way up the sides).*
Bake the crust for 25 minutes or until nice and crispy on the edge.

Lay the slices of Brie evenly on the potato crust and top with the diced ham.
In a small bowl, beat the eggs and cream together.
Gently pour the egg mixture over the ham and cheese.
Bake for an additional 30 minutes or until the eggs are set. Enjoy!

Orange Fruit Salad

Serves 10-12

Aunt Sheryl

This is another staple of A. Sheryl's Easter brunch. One year she didn't make it. I was crushed and asked, "Where is the orange stuff?" It has been part of the buffet every year since. Thanks A. Sheryl!

Ingredients:
8 oz container Cool Whip
3 oz box Orange Gelatin
12 oz container Cottage Cheese, Small Curd
2- 8 oz cans Crushed Pineapple, drained
11 oz can Mandarin Oranges, drained

Add Cool Whip to a large bowl.
Sprinkle gelatin over the cool whip and stir.
Add all other ingredients and mix well.
Transfer to serving dish.
Chill for at least one hour.

Overnight French Toast

Serves 6-8

This is a "special treat" breakfast. It is sweet and delicious; each bite is like a little bit of heaven. And serving it with fresh berries just takes it over the top. It is very simple to make and since you can prepare most of it the night before you won't be stressed in the morning. I like to serve it when we have overnight company. It is also wonderful to serve as part of a buffet brunch.

Ingredients:
3 Eggs
¾ c Milk
½ c Half & Half
1 tsp Vanilla Extract
1 Baguette, cut diagonally into 1" thick slices

¼ c Butter (½ a stick)
½ c Brown Sugar
1 T Maple Syrup

Spray a 9x13 baking dish with non-stick cooking spray.
Crack eggs into a medium bowl and lightly beat.
Add milk, half & half and vanilla and whisk all together.
Dip each slice of bread into egg mixture, making sure it is thoroughly coated on both sides. Place each piece of dipped bread into prepared casserole dish, lying flat (I do kind of jam the pieces of bread in if I need to).
**You may not use all of the egg mix. You can spoon extra over the top of each slice after you have all the pieces in the baking dish but do not be alarmed if you have egg batter left over.*
Cover and refrigerate overnight.

The next morning…Preheat oven to 350
In a small, microwaveable bowl combine butter, sugar and maple syrup.
Microwave for 30 seconds then stir until well combined; if you need to microwave again, go ahead.
Spoon a little of the sugar mixture over each slice of bread (you may have sugar mix left over too).
Bake in preheated oven for about 40 minutes or until puffy and golden brown.
Let stand for 5 minutes; serve warm with fresh berries and syrup on the side.

Alternate Preparation:

I like the above method because each person gets his or her own lovely piece of French toast. However, you can also make this into more of a breakfast bread pudding.

Just cube the bread instead of slicing it, place it all in the prepared baking dish and pour the egg mixture over the bread. Then, press the bread cubes down so you know each piece is soaked with the egg mixture. Cover, refrigerate and proceed as described above.

With this method, it is a little bit faster to prepare and a little easier to serve to a big crowd since everyone can just scoop out the serving size they want. Perfect if you are serving as part of a brunch as opposed to the main breakfast item.

Perfect Boiled Eggs

Boiled eggs are a joke in my immediate family. My sister and I could NEVER remember how long to boil them depending on if we wanted them hard or soft-boiled. We called my mom EVERY time we wanted to boil an egg. And every time we called, my mom was beside herself that we couldn't remember. It was ridiculous (and hilarious)! But now, I have solved the mystery. And written it down which always helps.

Hard-Boiled Eggs
Gently place eggs in a pot and fill with cold water.
Put pot on stove over high heat and bring to a boil.
As soon as the water boils, remove from heat and cover.
Let the eggs sit, covered in the hot water for exactly 10 minutes.
Drain, cool by running under cold water, peel.
You will have the perfect hard-boiled egg ever time; no runny white, no gray yolk, just perfect!

Soft-Boiled Eggs
Put enough water in a pot that your eggs will be covered when you put them in later.
Bring the pot of water to a boil.
Gently put the (cold) eggs into the boiling water using a long handled spoon or a spider.
Boil eggs for exactly 6 minutes.

My favorite way to eat Soft-Boiled Eggs:
Butter a piece of soft bread.
Cut it into bite-sized pieces and put it in a flat bowl.
When you take your egg out of the water, cut it in half with a butter knife right over the bread so that the bread soaks up the yolk (be careful no little shell pieces fall in too).
Scoop out the egg white with a spoon, drop into the bowl and chop it up with a knife.
Sprinkle with salt and pepper.
Give a little stir and enjoy!

Quiche

Serves 8

Aunt Clare (from her Aunt Theresa)

I took a day to make this with Aunt Clare and it was so much fun! Although there are measurements below, she really doesn't measure anything (except the eggs and milk). She also doesn't know why the milk needs to be scalded but that is what her Aunt Theresa did, so that is what she does... I will follow suit. You can also fill this quiche with different ingredients if you want- swap out the broccoli for spinach; use bacon instead of ham. No matter what, it is delicious!

Ingredients:
9" Pie Shell, half-baked*
2 oz Broccoli, blanched or steamed
1½ oz cubed Ham
1 heaping tsp finely chopped Onions
2 heaping T cubed Tomatoes
6 oz Swiss Cheese, shredded
1 cup Milk, scalded (see below)
4 Eggs, slightly beaten
½ tsp Salt
¼ tsp Pepper
dash Nutmeg
2 T chopped Parsley, divided

Preheat oven to 450 degrees
Place your piecrust in your pie plate and crimp the edges.
Bake in the oven for about 10 minutes to prebake (see below).

Meanwhile, blanch broccoli in 2 cups of boiling, salted water until tender (about 3-4 minutes).
Drain broccoli; set aside until cool enough to handle.
To scald milk, bring it almost to a boil then remove from heat and let cool a bit.

Cut broccoli into small, bite-sized pieces.
Layer broccoli, ham, tomatoes, onions and cheese in a half-baked pastry shell.
Mix milk, eggs, seasonings and half of the parsley together (if the milk is too hot it will cook the eggs).
Pour egg mixture into the pastry shell.
Bake for 10 minutes and then reduce the temperature to 325; continue to bake 30-35 minutes.
Check for doneness by sticking a knife in the center; if it comes out clean, it's done.
Remove from oven and let stand a few minutes before serving.
Sprinkle the top with the remaining parsley.

***Half Baked Pie Shell-** the best way to do this is to "blind bake" the crust first. Put the pie crust in your dish and finish the edges as you normally would. Then, place a piece of foil or parchment paper on top of the crust. Fill with pie weights, uncooked rice or dry beans (I reuse the same beans over and over). Bake for about 10-15 minutes or until the crust is half-baked. Remove the foil/parchment with the weights/beans and proceed with the recipe.

If you don't blind bake with weights your piecrust will puff on the bottom and fall on the sides; keep your eye on it. It won't look as pretty but it will still taste just as good. A. Clare said her piecrust almost always falls when she half-bakes it but it still tastes delicious so it doesn't matter. I've never noticed in all my life that her crust falls so I think she is on to something here!

Sausage Gravy

Serves 6-8

I tried to make biscuits and gravy so many times at home and it never worked out. It would taste like flour or just be a big ball of paste. It was actually a huge improvement when it was the right consistency but just didn't have any flavor. I remember it was my 5th attempt and I decided, "This is it! If it doesn't work this time I will just order these at restaurants." Luckily, 5th time was the charm! And I like mine better than any restaurant version!

Ingredients:
1 lb Breakfast Sausage
3 T Butter
¼ c Flour
2 c Milk, warmed if possible
2/3 c low sodium Chicken Stock
¼ tsp Pepper
pinch of Salt (if necessary)

Brown the sausage in a large pan over medium-high heat, cast iron if you have it.
Scoot the sausage to the edges of the pan and melt the butter in the middle.
Add the flour to the melted butter and stir together.
Continue to stir everything together and cook for at least another minute or two.
Cooking the flour like this will get rid of the "raw flour" taste.

While stirring constantly, slowly pour in the milk.
Continue to stir until combined.
Add the chicken stock and blend together.
Add pepper.
Turn the heat down if you haven't already.

Continue to stir.
The gravy will thicken as it continues to simmer.
Taste and adjust seasoning as necessary.
You can thin out with splashes of milk or extra splashes of chicken stock if needed.

Serve hot over warm biscuits.
Even better if you top with an over-easy egg… mmmmm…..

Smoked Salmon Spread

Makes 1½ Cups

This is a great cream cheese based spread and an ideal way to stretch your dollar. It is a sophisticated addition to any cocktail party served with crackers and I love to use it for brunch too!

Ingredients:
8 oz brick Cream Cheese, softened
4 oz Smoked Salmon, chopped
3 dashes Worcestershire Sauce
2 dashes Tabasco Sauce
1 tsp chopped Dill
1 Green Onion, chopped

Stir softened cream cheese in a bowl until workable.
Add the remaining ingredients; mix until combined and all ingredients are evenly distributed.
Keep chilled until ready to serve.

If serving for breakfast or brunch, have a basket of bagels and a platter filled with thin slices of cucumbers, tomatoes, red onions and capers. People can make their own version of "bagels and lox."

Breads

Banana Bread

Blueberry Biscuit Bread

Maple Bacon Scones

Sue's Monkey Bread

Zucchini Bread

Banana Bread/Cake

2 Loaves or 1 Bundt

Aunt Sheryl (her Great Aunt Lois' recipe)

This is so, so good. People I have made it for say it is the best banana bread they have ever had. As the name implies, it really can be a cake (frost with cream cheese frosting). But, if it is a cake then I would feel guilty eating it for breakfast. As a bread, however, I can have a few slices with my tea in the morning completely guilt free.

Ingredients:
2 c Flour
2 tsp Baking Powder
½ tsp Baking Soda
½ tsp Salt
1 tsp Ground Cinnamon
1 c Butter, softened (2 sticks)
1½ c Sugar
2 Eggs, beaten
1 tsp Vanilla
1 c mashed Bananas (3-4 very ripe bananas)
½ c Milk

Preheat oven to 350
Spray loaf pans or Bundt pan lightly with nonstick cooking spray.

In a medium bowl, sift together the first 5 ingredients.
In a large mixing bowl, cream the butter with an electric hand mixer.
Add the sugar gradually while beating with the mixer.
Add eggs and beat thoroughly.
Add banana and vanilla, beat thoroughly.
Add milk alternating with dry ingredients; begin and end with the milk.
Pour batter into prepared pans and bake until a toothpick comes out clean; about 45-60 minutes.

Blueberry Biscuit Bread

1 Loaf

This is not your regular quick bread; it really is more like a big biscuit. It is yummy to serve for breakfast, with tea or just as a snack. It is lovely sliced with a little bit of butter spread on top. But, I love it when it gets really toasted... then spread some butter on top.

Ingredients:
3 c Flour
1/3 c Sugar
1 T Baking Powder
1 tsp Baking Soda
1 tsp Salt
1 ¾ c Buttermilk
1 Egg, lightly beaten
¼ c Butter, melted
½ pint Blueberries

Preheat oven to 325
Grease a loaf pan.

In a large mixing bowl, sift together the first 5 ingredients.
In a small bowl, whisk together the egg and buttermilk.
Add the buttermilk mixture all at once to the flour and begin to combine just until moistened.
Just before the mixture is all the way moistened add the blueberries and gently fold.
Add the melted butter and continue to fold just until everything is combined.
Pour into a greased loaf pan.
Bake for 55 minutes or until a toothpick comes out clean.

Cool on a wire rack for 10 minutes in the pan, then remove from pan and leave on rack until completely cooled.
Wrap in foil to store.
I usually wait until the next day to cut into it and it is delicious!

Maple Bacon Scones

Serves 8

I love scones. They are easy to make, absolutely delicious and make me feel very proper… while at the same time being very comforting. I started off with a very basic scone recipe and just started adding ingredients when I wanted to change the flavors. This particular flavor combo was such a hit that I felt the need to share it with you. Keys to scones: 1. Work fast, you want the butter to stay cold and 2. Don't overwork the dough, handle it as little as possible. Scones are definitely best on the day they are baked but not too shabby the next day if you warm them up in the oven for a few minutes. Enjoy!

Ingredients:
2 c Flour
1 T Baking Powder
½ tsp Salt
2 T Brown Sugar
5 T Cold Butter, diced
4 pieces cooked Bacon, crumbled
2½ T Maple Syrup
¾ c + 2 T (or 7 oz) Heavy Cream, plus extra for brushing

Preheat oven to 400
Line a baking sheet with parchment paper.

Sift first 4 ingredients into a bowl.
Add butter to the bowl and "cut" in using a pastry blender or two butter knives until the butter is the size of peas.
Add the bacon and toss a bit.
Add the syrup and cream; stir just until combined.

Dump the dough onto a lightly floured work surface.
Using your hands, form the dough into a 1 – 1½" thick disc.
Cut into 8 equal triangles.
Place the scones on the prepared baking sheet.
Lightly brush the tops of the scones with more heavy cream.
Bake until golden brown, about 18-20 minutes.

Sue's Monkey Bread

1 Bundt

I actually got this recipe from my friend Cyndi but I know it was her mom, Sue, who first made it for us. I remember the first time I had it, I was about 8 and it was like heaven! This is just fun and a great recipe to make with kids.

Ingredients:
3 cans of Pillsbury Original Biscuits (not Grands)
3 tsp Cinnamon
1 c Granulated Sugar
8 T Butter (1 stick)
1 c Brown Sugar

Preheat oven to 350
Grease a Bundt pan.

Take each biscuit and cut into quarters.
Mix the cinnamon and granulated sugar together in a small bowl.
Roll each piece of biscuit in the cinnamon and sugar mixture.

Melt butter in a small saucepan.
Add brown sugar and stir until you have a smooth "sauce" consistency.

Think of each can as a layer.
Place one layer of cinnamon/sugar coated biscuits in the prepared Bundt pan and pour 1/3 of the sauce over the biscuits*.
Repeat layers.

Bake in the oven for about 30 minutes.
Let cool in pan for 10 minutes then flip onto a serving plate.
Everyone can just pull off the number of pieces (read: giant hunk) they want.

*If you want you can add nuts to the Monkey Bread. Just sprinkle nuts on in between each layer.

Zucchini Bread 2 Loaves

Based on a recipe from Aunt Joy

I LOVE quick breads. I LOVE zucchini. I'll let you guess how I feel about this! Like all quick breads, this freezes great!

Ingredients:

3 c Flour
1 tsp Salt
1 tsp Baking Soda
¼ tsp Baking Powder
1½ tsp Cinnamon
1 c Vegetable Oil
2 c Sugar
3 Eggs
1 T Vanilla Extract
2 medium Zucchini, grated

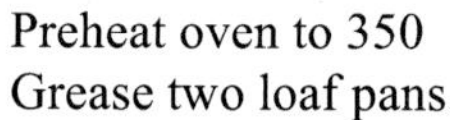

Preheat oven to 350
Grease two loaf pans.

In a medium bowl, sift together the first 5 ingredients.
In a large mixing bowl, using an electric hand mixer, beat together the oil and sugar.
Add the eggs to the oil/sugar mixture one at a time, beating thoroughly after each addition.
Add vanilla and beat.
Stir in zucchini with a spatula.
Add dry ingredients and stir just until combined, don't over mix!

Pour batter into prepared loaf pans and bake until a toothpick inserted into the center comes out clean, about 1 hour.

Let cool in pans, on a rack, for 10 minutes.
Remove from pans and let cool completely.

Lunch

French Onion Soup & Steak Sandwich

Soups

Beef Barley Soup

Chicken Soup

Chili

Clam Chowder

French Onion Soup

Ham & Bean Soup

Roasted Carrot Soup

Beef Barley Soup

Serves 8 - 10

This might be my husband's favorite thing that I make. Definitely in the top 5. This is just a really good beefy soup and I LOVE the barley in it. It's a bowl full of coziness. Give it a try, you won't be sorry.

Ingredients:
1 T Olive Oil
2¼ - 2½ lbs boneless Short Ribs
Salt & Pepper
1 Leek, chopped (white and light green parts only)
5 medium Carrots, diced
1 large Onion, chopped
3 stalks Celery, chopped
4 cloves Garlic, minced
8 c Beef Stock
2 c Chicken Stock
2 sprigs Thyme
3 Bay Leaves
1 c Pearled Barley
½ c Parsley, chopped

Heat oil in a Dutch Oven over medium-high heat.
Season the short ribs on both sides with salt & pepper.
Brown the short ribs on both sides, in batches if necessary (you don't want to crowd the pan). You want the short ribs really BROWNED, not gray. It will probably take at least 10 minutes per side.
Remove short ribs from pot; set aside.
Remove all but 2 tablespoons of fat from the pot.
Add the leeks, carrots, onion and celery to the pot.
Sprinkle the veggies with a little salt and pepper and sauté, stirring often, until they begin to soften; about 10 minutes.
Add the garlic and stir constantly for 1 minute.
Pour in the beef and chicken stocks.
Add the thyme and bay leaves to the pot.
Bring to a boil then reduce to a simmer.
Cut the short ribs into bite-sized pieces; return the short ribs and any juices that have collected to the pot.
Continue to simmer for 1 hour.

Meanwhile, in a separate pot bring 4 cups of water to a boil.
Add the barley to the pot of boiling water; simmer uncovered for 30 minutes.
Drain the barley and set aside.

After the soup has been simmering for an hour, remove the thyme stems.
Add the barley to the pot.
Continue to cook for an additional 20 minutes so all the flavors can combine.
Remove the bay leaves.
Add ¾ of the parsley at the very end and stir.
Taste and adjust seasonings if necessary.

Divide the soup into bowls and garnish each bowl with a little more fresh parsley.

Chicken Soup

Serves 8-10

I have heard this was my Grandpa Inchiostro's recipe. I have heard it's my Grandma Inchiostro's recipe. I always remember eating it at my Aunt May's house. I know my Dad, sister and I all make it. I'm sure if you ate the four different bowls, they would all taste a little different. I am also sure that one of these four bowls, whichever you prefer, will be the best chicken soup you have ever had. It is DELICIOUS! It makes you feel better when you are sick, cozy when it is cold and happy any other time of the year because it is just that good.

Ingredients:
1 Chicken
1 T Salt, plus more for cleaning/rinsing
1 ½ tsp Pepper
2 tsp Garlic Powder
1/3 cup chopped Parsley, divided
1 medium Onion, chopped
3 stalks of Celery, chopped
5 med to large Carrots- 2 whole, 3 chopped
1-2 Chicken Bouillon Cubes
1 cup Acini de Pepe Noodles, uncooked
1 Egg
2/3 cup grated Parmesan Cheese

Clean chicken thoroughly inside and out with cold water.
Liberally salt the cavity of chicken and then rinse out.
Season the cavity of the chicken with 1 tablespoon of salt, the pepper, garlic powder and the parsley (less 2-3 tablespoons).
Place seasoned chicken in a large stockpot and fill with cold water until the water covers the chicken by an inch.
Add onions, celery and two whole carrots to the pot.
Bring to a boil then lower to a simmer.
Simmer for about an hour and a half.
**The chicken floats to the top so I usually flip it over every 30 - 45 minutes to make sure it is evenly cooked.*
Add the chopped carrots and simmer for another 45 minutes.

Remove the whole carrots, chop, return to pot.
Remove the chicken and let it cool enough to handle.
Skin, debone and cube or shred the chicken.

Taste the broth for flavor and adjust seasonings if necessary; I usually add 1 bouillon cube.
**You will be adding Parmesan cheese later, which is salty so keep that in mind.*
Add the Acini de Pepe noodles to the pot and continue to simmer.

While the noodles are cooking, beat the egg in a medium sized bowl.
<u>Slowly</u> add some of the hot broth to the egg while constantly beating.
Add the Parmesan cheese to the egg and beat all together.
Then, continue to slowly add even more broth to the egg mixture.

**You will add at least a cup of broth before you are finished. You want to slowly bring the temperature of the egg mixture up. If you add a cold egg to a hot pot, the egg will cook as soon as it hits the heat. So, you want to temper the egg.*

After you have brought the temperature of the egg mixture up, gradually add it to the pot while stirring constantly.

Add the chicken back to the pot.
**I like my soup more noodley so I only use ½ of the chicken. You put in however much you want.*
Add the remaining parsley.
Stir everything to combine.
Ladle into bowls.
Have some grated Parmesan cheese on the table and people can add extra to their bowl if they would like.

Note: The soup will thicken as it sits in the fridge because the noodles will continue to absorb the broth. As you heat the soup up again it will thin. If it is still too thick for you add some water while heating. Personally, I love how thick it gets the second day.

Option: A. May takes about 1/3 of the broth and puts it in a separate pot. She cooks the noodles in that broth and adds the egg/cheese mix directly to the noodles. She keeps the noodles in one dish, the chicken in a second dish and the broth in another. This way the noodles do not continue to absorb the broth. It is delicious and everyone can create their own consistency or noodle to chicken to broth ratio. I am too lazy for these extra steps, which is why I make everything in one pot.

Chili Serves 12

Dad

This is just a great chili recipe; warm, hearty and comforting. We don't like too much spice so it isn't spicy but you can always punch up the heat if you want. You can easily cut this recipe in half but it is really just as easy to make a giant batch, so why not? Freeze it in family size serving portions and you can eat from one batch over and over again.

Ingredients:
Olive Oil
1 lb Ground Pork
2 lbs Ground Chuck (you can use 3lbs of beef if you choose)
1 ½ tsp Salt
¾ tsp Pepper
2 T Chili Powder, divided
1 large or 2 medium Onions, chopped
6 large cloves Garlic, minced
6 oz can Tomato Paste
15 oz can Tomato Sauce
2- 28 oz cans Diced or Petite Diced Tomatoes
2- 40 oz cans prepared Chili Beans (I like Brooks)
½ tsp Cayenne Pepper (optional)

Heat a few tablespoons of oil in a large pot on medium-high to high heat.
Add pork; begin to brown and break into very small pieces.
Cook for about 3 minutes.
Add beef; season with salt, pepper and 1 tablespoon of chili powder.
Stir everything together and continue to brown and break into small pieces for another 5 minutes.
Add onions to soften in beef-pork mixture; cook and stir occasionally for another 5 minutes.
Add garlic and stir for 30 seconds.
Add tomato paste; stir until well combined and brown the tomato paste for 2 minutes.
Add another tablespoon of chili powder and mix together.
Add cans of tomato sauce, diced tomatoes and chili beans; do not drain any of the cans first.
Add cayenne pepper if desired.

Bring to a full rolling boil stirring frequently.
Reduce heat to a simmer.
Taste and add chili powder as necessary.
Simmer uncovered at least 15 minutes, stirring frequently, or until it reaches the desired consistency.
You can add water if it is too thick.

Clam Chowder

Serves 12

Grandma Babor/Mom

This entire book was created because I want to hold on to family traditions. As important as they all are to me, none of them are quite as "specific" as this one. I don't think I could have Christmas Eve with my family without Clam Chowder (and ham). It has been going on for at least half a century and I know it will continue as long as I am here. Some people like to top it with Tabasco but I like to serve it with some crumbled bacon on top. Takes it to a whole new level... mmmmm....

Ingredients:

8 T Butter (1 stick)
1 large Onion, chopped
6 cans Campbell's Cream of Potato Soup
3 cans Campbell's New England Clam Chowder
½ gallon of Half & Half
8- 6½ oz cans of Minced Clams, don't drain
Crumbled Bacon, for garnish (optional)

Preheat oven to 200
On the stove, melt the butter in a Dutch oven over medium heat.
Add the onion and sauté until soft, about 10-15 minutes.
Add all remaining ingredients to the pot and mix together.
Place in the oven, cover and bake at 200 degrees for 4-6 hours, stirring at least every 30 minutes.
Add salt and pepper to taste.

Below are ingredients for the pared down version (serves 3-4):
2 cans Cream of Potato
1 can NE Clam Chowder
1 small Onion, chopped
1/3 stick Butter
2 2/3 cups Half & Half
3 cans Minced Clams, don't drain

French Onion Soup

Serves 6-8

This recipe is heavily influenced by my Great-Uncle Doc. I asked him for his delicious French Onion Soup recipe and I just kept tweaking little things. It is very easy to make and just as good (if not significantly better) than what you would order in a café. And, you can probably make an entire pot at home for what you pay for one bowl in a restaurant.

Ingredients:
2 T Butter
1 T Olive Oil
3 lbs Yellow Onions, sliced or diced to your liking*
Salt & Pepper
6 c Beef Stock
3 sprigs Thyme
2 bay leaves
1 T Worcestershire Sauce
Heavy splash Medium-Dry Sherry (optional)

Additional (Optional) Ingredients:
Toasted Baguette Slices
Grated Gruyere Cheese

**I slice my onions in a half moon shape and then slice in half again. I feel this way they still look pretty but aren't sliding off the spoon because they are so long.*

Heat butter and olive oil in a pot over medium to medium-high heat.
Add onions, season with some salt and pepper.
Cook onions, stirring often, until caramelized; about 20 minutes.
Add stock, thyme, bay leaves, Worcestershire and sherry; stir everything together.
Bring to a boil then reduce to a simmer; simmer for 30 minutes.
Remove thyme stems and bay leaves.
Taste and adjust seasonings if necessary.

You can eat as is or you can bump it up a notch…
Ladle into broiler-safe bowls.
Top with homemade croutons or toasted baguette slices and grated Gruyere cheese.
Broil until cheese browns and bubbles.
Ooey, gooey deliciousness!

Ham & Bean Soup

Serves 8

This is the perfect soup to make after Christmas... or after Easter... or anytime after you have baked a bone-in ham. If you aren't sure what to do with that bone but you don't want to waste all that delicious ham, make some Ham & Bean Soup. You won't be sorry!

Ingredients:

4 c Great Northern Beans
Ham Bone
1 medium Onion, chopped
2 stalks Celery, chopped
3 medium Carrots, chopped
Salt & Pepper
¼ c Parsley, chopped

Rinse and sort 4 cups of great Northern beans.
Place small hambone in a pot and cover with water; add beans.
Bring to boil; reduce to simmer.
Simmer with the lid on a tilt for two hours.

Add the onion, celery and carrots; simmer for another hour.
Remove ham bone 30 min after you have added the veggies to the soup; set aside until cool enough to handle.
Pull meat off the bone and cut or shred into pieces.

After soup has cooked for at least three hours and the beans are tender, use an immersion blender to puree the mixture a little; only put it in there for about 15 seconds.
Return the pulled ham to the pot, stir and season with salt and pepper as needed.
Stir in half of the parsley and ladle into bowls.
Garnish each bowl with a little more parsley.

Roasted Carrot Soup

Serves 2-4

Roasting the carrots caramelizes them and really brings out their natural sweetness. We like this soup quite thick but if you want a thinner consistency just add a little extra stock. Speaking of stock, you could easily make this soup vegan/vegetarian by switching out the Chicken Stock with Vegetable Stock. You can also make the soup ahead of time, store in the fridge and reheat before serving. So simple!

Ingredients:

1½ lbs Carrots (about 6-8 carrots)
Olive Oil
4 small sprigs Thyme (plus more for garnish)
2 c low-sodium Chicken Stock
½ a small - medium Onion, chopped
1 large or 2 small cloves Garlic, minced
¼ tsp Ground Ginger

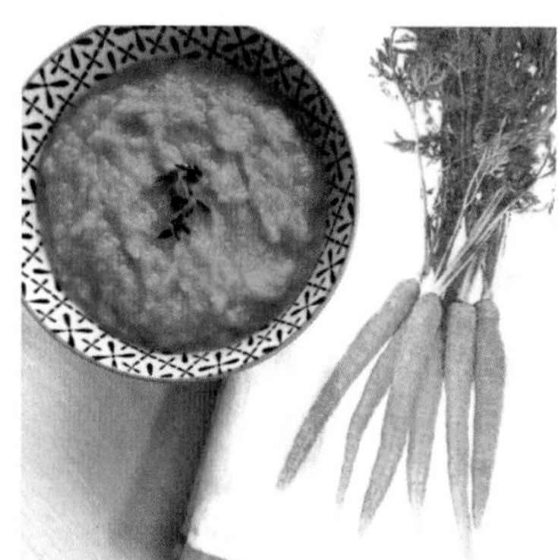

Preheat the oven to 425
Line a sheet pan with foil.
Peel the carrots and cut into 1½ " chunks.
Put carrots on prepared sheet pan; drizzle with olive oil and sprinkle with some salt and pepper.
Use your hands to toss and make sure everything is evenly coated.
Lay the thyme sprigs on the sheet pan.
Roast in the oven for 20 minutes; toss and roast another 15 minutes or until nice and caramelized.

In the meantime, in a medium pot over medium heat, drizzle another tablespoon of olive oil.
Add onions and sprinkle with a little salt and pepper.
Cook until translucent, stirring occasionally (about 7 minutes).
Add garlic and stir constantly for 30 seconds.
Add chicken stock and let come to a simmer.

When the carrots are ready, remove the thyme stems then add the roasted carrots to the pot.
Add the ground ginger and stir.
Let simmer for 5 minutes.
Use an immersion blender to puree the soup.
**If you don't have an immersion blender use a regular blender and puree in batches holding a towel over the lid. Don't fill blender more than a third of the way.*
Serve warm and garnish with some fresh thyme.

Salads

Caesar Salad

Cucumber Tomato Salad

Mom's Salad

Salad Niçoise

Strawberry Spinach Salad

Caesar Salad

Serves 4-6

Aunt Joy

I know A. Joy is sick of making this salad. She has to make it for most family gatherings but it is just so delicious. We can't help but ask for it! My sister even asked for her to make it for her college graduation party.... in Wyoming! She drove 16 hours. Aunt Joy is the best!

Ingredients:
1 head Romaine Lettuce
Caesar Salad Dressing (see below)
¼ c grated Parmesan Cheese
Freshly ground pepper to taste
1 c Onion & Garlic Croutons

Tear washed and dried romaine into fork sized pieces and place in a salad bowl.
Pour over dressing and toss lightly.
Add cheese, pepper and croutons.
Toss until well distributed.

Caesar Salad Dressing
Ingredients:
1 clove Garlic, crushed
¼ tsp Mustard
1/8 tsp Worcestershire sauce
2 Tbsp Lemon Juice
1/3 c Olive Oil
1 Egg (well-beaten)

In a shallow bowl, smash the garlic clove with a fork.
Add the mustard and Worcestershire sauce and mix all together.
Stir in lemon juice and olive oil.
Stir in 1 well-beaten egg.

**Aunt Joy will make the dressing a day or two ahead of time for the flavors to blend together. She removes the garlic clove before dressing the salad.*

She omits anchovy for personal preference. If you want to add it, mash up 6 anchovy fillets along with the garlic clove or add 1 tsp of anchovy paste.

Cucumber & Tomato Salad

Serves 4

This salad is so light and refreshing. It is quick and easy to make and is a great side dish to so many main courses, especially a "heavy" main course. Great with Brian's Lamb Lollipops (pg. 91), Ribs (pg. 97) and Barbecued Chicken (pg. 86) just to name a few.

Ingredients:
1 pint Grape Tomatoes
2/3 – ¾ of an English Cucumber
¾ tsp Salt
¼ tsp Pepper
1 T Red Wine Vinegar
2 tsp Olive Oil

Slice the tomatoes in half, put in a bowl.
Cut the cucumber in half lengthwise, scoop out the seeds with a spoon.
Slice the cucumber so the pieces are about the same size as the tomato halves, add to bowl.
Sprinkle with the salt and pepper.
Pour the vinegar and olive oil over the top; toss everything together.
Let sit for at least 20 minutes at room temperature, tossing occasionally.
Taste for seasonings and serve.

Variations:
I like the simplest version but you can add one or all of the following: thinly sliced red onions, crumbled feta cheese, Kalamata olives and/or fresh mint.

Mom's Salad

Serves 8-10

Mom

These are my mom's exact directions. Notice no measurements. It's ok, that means it's the perfect opportunity to make it your own. For example, I only use the dark and light green parts of the green onion and I start with 2 tablespoons each of balsamic vinegar and olive oil. I know she uses all dried herbs but if you want to use fresh, feel free. This salad is easy and delicious and goes with everything!

Ingredients:
1 large head Romaine lettuce
3 Green Onions, chopped
Garlic Powder
Pepper
Italian Seasoning
Dried Basil
Dried Oregano
Dried Rosemary
Balsamic Vinegar
Olive Oil

Wash and dry lettuce and break into pieces.
Add the green onions.
Sprinkle with the next 6 ingredients (like you would salt & pepper); toss.
Pour balsamic vinegar and olive oil over the top; toss until everything is evenly coated.

You can add tomatoes, Parmesan cheese (mom always adds parm), anything you want to this; just practice on how much seasoning you like.

Salade Niçoise

Serves 3-4

*I absolutely **love** this salad. I didn't know if I should put it in the "salad" category, because it is a salad, or the "main courses" category because it is absolutely an entire meal. I do know that any time I make this it feels like a special occasion. It is just too beautiful not to think of it as such. It is not hard to make but it has a lot of ingredients and there are a lot of steps. But, trust me when I say it is totally worth it. Serve with a deliciously crusty piece of bread and a nice, crisp white wine. Enjoy!*

Ingredients:

Vinaigrette:
2 tsp minced Garlic
1 tsp Dijon Mustard
3 T Red Wine Vinegar
2 T fresh Lemon Juice
¼ c chopped Parsley
½ tsp low-sodium Soy Sauce
¼ tsp Salt
¼ tsp Pepper
½ c Extra-Virgin Olive Oil

Salad:
½ lb Teeny Tiny Potatoes
2 Eggs, Hard-Boiled (pg. 21) and quartered
½ lb Green Beans
1 lb Tuna Steak (I like yellow fin/ahi)
Extra-virgin Olive Oil
Salt & Pepper
Romaine Lettuce, chopped (or one 9oz bag of lettuce)
½ pint Grape Tomatoes
¼ cup pitted Niçoise olives

Put all the ingredients for the vinaigrette in a jar and shake.
**This will emulsify the vinaigrette. Make sure you have a secure lid. I usually hold a paper towel over the top of the lid just in case.*
If you don't have a good jar to use just put the first 6 ingredients in a bowl and whisk in the olive oil.
Set vinaigrette aside while you prepare the ingredients for the salad.
**You will not use all the vinaigrette; there will be plenty left over. This is a thin dressing so a little goes a long way. Don't use too much!*

This salad is truly arranged. I prepare each ingredient separately, dress it separately, and then arrange it on each individual plate or on one big platter.

Potatoes- Put the teeny tiny potatoes in a pot of cold water and bring to a boil.
Add a lot of salt to the water once it boils and continue to boil until potatoes are cooked, about 10 minutes.
Drain and put back in hot pot.
Drizzle a little of the vinaigrette on them, toss and set aside.

Green Beans- I am guilty of using the green beans that come in a bag. It is just so much easier sometimes. I cook the green beans in the steamer bag in the microwave for about 3 ½ minutes and leave them in the bag until I am ready to dress them. I use about ½ of the bag.

Tuna- Heat a pan on the stove over medium-high to high heat.
Rub tuna steak(s) with olive oil and season with salt and pepper.
Place the tuna in the hot pan and sear it; about 1½ - 2 minutes per side.
**Of course, if you don't like it rare, cook your tuna longer... but in my humble opinion, you are missing out.*

While the tuna is searing you can start arranging all the ingredients.
I usually get one big bowl and take turns tossing each ingredient with a little bit of dressing:
Toss lettuce with some dressing and then divide among plates.
Toss tomatoes with dressing, and then divide among plates… and so on and so forth with the olives, green beans and potatoes.

Arrange the eggs on each plate and drizzle some vinaigrette on top.
Slice the tuna and place right in the middle of the salad, then drizzle with a little more vinaigrette.

Look at your beautiful masterpiece!

Strawberry Spinach Salad

Serves 4-6

This salad is simple, delicious and it tastes like summer. Pairs great with anything grilled whether it's a Monte Cristo (pg. 53) or Barbecued Chicken (pg. 86).

Ingredients:
1½ T Olive Oil
1½ T White Wine Vinegar
1½ tsp Sugar
Dash Paprika
1 tsp Sesame Seeds, toasted
¾ tsp Poppy Seeds
pinch of Salt
8 oz Spinach
1 c sliced Strawberries

In a small bowl, whisk together the first 7 ingredients; set aside.

In a large salad bowl, add spinach and strawberries.
Pour dressing over and toss everything together.

Optional add-ins: Goat Cheese (*highly recommended*)
Red Onions
Toasted Almonds or Walnuts
Blueberries

Sandwiches

Croque Madame

Cuban Sandwich

Fried Chicken Sandwich

Monte Cristo

Rare Roast Beef

Steak Sandwich

The Perfect Burger

Croque Madame

2 Sandwiches

These look complicated but once you get the hang of it they are really quite simple and so very delicious. The hardest part is grating the cheese. If you grate one 6 oz hunk of cheese you will have plenty for both the sauce and the sandwiches. If you buy it already grated there really aren't any excuses. Serve with Mom's Salad (pg. 44) or your favorite lettuce tossed with the vinaigrette from the Salade Niçoise (pg. 45).

Ingredients:

Mornay Sauce:
½ T Butter
scant 1T Flour
½ cup Milk, warmed
¼ tsp Salt
dash of Pepper
pinch of Nutmeg
¼ cup grated Gruyere cheese

Sandwiches:
2 big or 4 small slices great bread (I like a French Country White)
Dijon Mustard
2-4 thin slices of Ham
½ cup grated Gruyere cheese
2 Eggs, over easy, sunny side up or poached

Preheat broiler

Mornay Sauce:
In a small saucepan, melt the butter.
Add the flour and stir constantly.
Let the butter/flour mix (roux) cook for a couple of minutes to get rid of the raw flour taste.

Slowly pour in the milk while whisking constantly.
Continue whisking until sauce is thickened (about 5 minutes).
Add salt, pepper and nutmeg.
Remove the saucepan from the heat and add the Gruyere; stir until you have a smooth sauce.

Sandwiches:
Toast each piece of bread.
Put a skillet on the stove over medium heat.

Spread a thin layer of mustard on each slice of toast.
Top each slice with a piece or two of ham.
Spread some Mornay sauce on top of the ham
Sprinkle the top with Gruyere cheese.

Place each open-faced sandwich on a parchment lined baking sheet.
Broil for 3-5 minutes until the cheese is bubbly.

In the meantime, cook your eggs over-easy or sunny side up (anything with a runny yolk).

Remove the sandwiches from the broiler, top with fried egg and serve immediately with a knife and fork.

Cuban Sandwich (Cubano)

2 Sandwiches

Preparing this sandwich is more like gathering ingredients than cooking. I get the pulled pork from a great BBQ place (Sugarfire), I get the rolls from a local bakery (Breadsmiths) and I usually get the ham from the deli counter at my local grocery store (I recommend Bavarian or Off-The-Bone). If you can't find a Cuban Bread Roll you can use a hoagie, ciabatta or even a hamburger bun. Serve with plantain chips or potato chips and some fresh pineapple.

Ingredients:
2 Cuban Bread Rolls
½ lb Pulled Pork
4 thinly sliced pieces of Ham
4 slices of Swiss Cheese
Dill Pickle slices
Yellow Mustard

Slice your rolls in half.
Spread a thin layer of mustard on each half of the bread.
On the bottom half of each roll layer:
- 1 slice of Swiss cheese
- half of the pulled pork
- 2 slices of ham
- pickles
- another slice of Swiss

Put the top layer of bread on your sandwich.

If you have a panini press, use it here.
I do not have one so I put a piece of foil on top of the sandwich and "press" it by putting a teakettle filled with water on top; a heavy pan works too.
The bread I use doesn't need to be buttered on the outside before it is grilled, yours might, especially if it is a bit soft on the outside.
Grill your sandwich on medium heat for about 5 minutes per side or until the sandwich is hot and the cheese is nice and melty.

Take your sandwich out of the pan and let it rest for a minute or so.
Then, I like to slice ours in half because the rolls are quite big but that is just my preference.

Fried Chicken Sandwich

4 Sandwiches

This one is just a winner!

Ingredients:
4 – 5oz skinless, boneless Chicken Breasts or Chicken Thighs
1 c Buttermilk
1½ tsp Dijon Mustard
½ tsp Salt
½ tsp Pepper
½ tsp Cayenne Pepper

1 c Flour
1½ tsp Baking Powder
1½ tsp Garlic Powder
1½ tsp Onion Powder
Vegetable Oil for Frying (up to 5 cups)

4 Sandwich Buns (rec Brioche), toasted
Shredded Lettuce
4 slices of Tomatoes (optional)
Sliced Dill Pickles
Mayonnaise

Whisk together the buttermilk, mustard, salt, pepper and cayenne pepper in a bowl.
Place the chicken pieces in a large Ziploc bag and pour the marinade over.
Make sure all the chicken is coated in the marinade.
Then, squeeze out the excess air and seal the bag.
Leave in the refrigerator for 2-8 hours.

When you are ready to cook the chicken, start heating your vegetable oil in a large frying pan (cast iron if you have it) over medium-high heat.
You want the oil hot but you don't want it to burn.

In another large plastic bag, combine the flour, baking powder, garlic powder and onion powder.
Close the bag and shake to mix it well.
Remove one piece of chicken from the marinade and let it drain off a bit.
Place that piece of chicken in the bag with the flour mixture; shake to ensure it is completely covered.
Carefully take out the coated chicken piece and begin frying it in the hot oil.
Continue to repeat these steps with the remaining chicken pieces.

**You can do a double batter if you want. Just put each chicken piece from the marinade, to the flour, back into the marinade again and back into the flour again. It will be delicious but I just don't find it necessary. For us, one batter dip is enough.*

Fry each piece of chicken for about 7-10 minutes per side.
When they are finished frying, place the chicken pieces on a large brown paper grocery bag to let some of the oil drain off.
Immediately sprinkle with a little extra salt.

Assembling the Sandwich:

1. Toast sandwich buns by spreading a little butter on each half and broiling them for a couple of minutes in the oven. You can skip this step but it is nice to have that buttery roll with a little crunch.
2. On the bottom half of the bun place the fried chicken, then top with shredded lettuce and pickles; tomato would be a good addition when in season.
3. Spread some mayo on the top half of the bun and put it on.
4. Enjoy!

Monte Cristo Sandwich

4 Sandwiches

This is just delightful. Please don't skip the Blackberry Jam. I know it sounds a little weird but just try it. If you don't like it you don't have to eat it again but I think you will be pleasantly surprised.

Ingredients:
3 Eggs
¼ c Milk
8 slices good White Bread
Mayonnaise
Dijon Mustard
8 slices Gouda
8 thin slices Ham
Blackberry Jam for serving

Whisk together the eggs and milk in a shallow dish, set aside.

Heat a pan on the stove over medium heat.

Lay out your 8 slices of bread in two rows of four- the top row being the top slice of each sandwich, the bottom row being the bottom slice of each.
Spread a thin layer of mayonnaise on the bottom row of bread and a thin layer of Dijon mustard on the top row of bread.

Put a slice of Gouda cheese on each slice of the bread on the bottom row.
Layer two slices of ham on top of the cheese, top with another slice of Gouda and then the top slice of bread.
Now you have 4 sandwiches.

Carefully dip each sandwich in the egg mixture letting is soak in a bit on both sides.
Put onto the heated, greased pan.
Cook until the cheese is melted and the egg batter has cooked to resemble French toast, about 6 minutes per side.

Let the sandwich rest for one minute then slice on the diagonal.
Serve hot with a dollop of blackberry jam on the side for dipping.

Rare Roast Beef

Serves 4-6

Dad

I love roast beef. I think I asked for it for at least 3 years in a row for my birthday dinner. Roast beef served with mashed potatoes and green beans; that is a cozy meal. But, the best thing to do with a roast beef is make it extra rare and slice it for sandwiches. Just rare beef on good bread, you don't need anything else!

Ingredients:
3 lb Roast*
3 to 4 cloves of Garlic, split into 3rds lengthwise
Olive Oil
Salt & Pepper

**Choosing the Roast:*
Choose a top round, bottom round or sirloin tip. Look for whichever looks best that day with the most marbling (small flecks of fat running through the meat- a good thing).

Preheat oven to 450; rack in the center of the oven.

Slice small pockets all over the roast with the tip of a knife; make them about ½ inch long by ¾ inch deep.
Stuff pockets with the garlic slices.
Rub oil all over the roast.
Season all over with salt and pepper to taste.

Place roast on a rack in a roasting pan, fat side up; roast for 15 minutes.
Reduce heat to 325 degrees and continue to roast for another 45 minutes or until the center of the roast reads 130 on a meat thermometer (place the thermometer in the deepest part of the flesh).

Take out of oven, tent with foil and let stand at least 15 minutes.
Slice against the grain, as thinly as possible.

For Sandwiches:
Serve on wonderfully fresh crusty bread- a baguette or a good Italian/French loaf.

Steak Sandwich 2 Large Sandwiches

This is the sandwich that started a Vannoni family tradition. My husband loves sandwiches so I would make him a steak sandwich for special occasions (his birthday and Father's Day). It became such a "thing" that we decided those two weeks of the year would always be "Sandwich Week" and the Steak Sandwich is always the finale! I like to use Beef Tenderloin for this but you could just as easily use a Ribeye or Strip Steak (pg. 104).

Indgredients:
1 Vidalia Onion, sliced (half moon shape)
1 T Butter
1 T Olive Oil
½ tsp Salt
¼ tsp Pepper
1½ tsp Prepared Horseradish Cream
¼ c Mayonnaise (I always use Hellmann's)
1 lb Beef Tenderloin, prepared (pg. 88)
Baguette
Blue Cheese (a wedge sliced or crumbles)
Arugula

Caramelizing Onions:
On the stove, heat the butter and the olive oil in a large pan or shallow stock pot over medium to medium high heat.
When the butter is melted and the oil is hot, add the onion slices, salt and pepper.
Mix all together until everything is evenly coated and begin caramelizing the onions.
Cook for 20 minutes, stirring about every 2 minutes to make sure everything gets evenly cooked.
Turn the heat to medium-low and continue cooking (and stirring) for another 15 minutes.
When your onions are ready turn them to low just to keep warm.
**You can caramelize the onions ahead of time and heat them up in the microwave or on the stove when you are ready to assemble the sandwiches.*

While the onions are cooking you can prep other components of the sandwich.

In a bowl, mix the horseradish cream and mayo; keep in fridge until ready.
Put the baguette in a warm oven for about 5 minutes to get nice and crusty.
After you take out the bread, move the oven rack into the top 1/3 of the oven and turn it to broil.
Slice the meat into thin slices.

Assembly:
Slice the baguette into 6" portions for your two sandwiches, then down the middle horizontally.
Dip the bottom half of each sandwich piece in the meat juice (from slicing) and spread the top half of each sandwich with some of the mayo mixture.
Layer the meat on the bottom half of the sandwich.
Top with warm onions and blue cheese.
Place the bottom half of each sandwich on a foil lined baking sheet.
Put under broiler for about 2 minutes until the cheese melts; make sure you watch it so it doesn't burn.

Remove from oven, top with a heaping handful of arugula and the top piece of the baguette.

The Perfect Burger

Serves 6

That pretty much says it all. Just make sure you don't use "lean" ground beef; you want the flavor of ground chuck. Top your burger however you like. My perfect burger only needs three things: American cheese, arugula and mayo. Perfection! If you put it on a sweet Hawaiian roll or Brioche bun, even better!

Ingredients:
2 lbs Ground Chuck (80%/20%)
1 tsp Salt
1 tsp Pepper
1 tsp Garlic Powder
1 T Worcestershire sauce
1 Egg

Use large serving fork to lightly break meat up in a large mixing bowl.
Season beef with next four ingredients.
Crack egg into the side of the bowl and beat slightly with the large fork (the egg just helps hold the meat together).
Use the fork to mix everything just until incorporated.
Then, use your hands to get in there and make sure all is combined.
**You don't want to over handle the meat (while mixing and making into patties) or it will get tough.*

Lightly press meat down to evenly fill the bottom of the bowl.
Use your hand to evenly divide the one large patty into six "pie pieces".
**That way you will know each burger is about the same size (1/3 lb) and therefore they will all cook at the same time.*
Form each pie piece into a patty again, using as little handling as possible.

**Forming The Patty: The perfect patty is thinner in the middle and thicker at the edges. It is also larger than the bun you plan to put it on. Burgers plump up in the middle and shrink in diameter when they cook. If the patty is thinner in the middle and larger than the bun, after it is cooked, it will be of even thickness throughout and fit on the bun perfectly.*

Cook burgers on a hot grill or in a hot cast iron skillet.
If you like your burgers cooked to a medium doneness, grill for about 4 minutes with the lid closed, flip the burger (and add the cheese of your liking).
Grill for 4 more minutes with the lid closed.
Remove from grill and let the burgers rest for at least 5 minutes.

Dinner

Lamb Lollipops, Roasted Asparagus & Roasted Teeny Tiny Potatoes

Appetizers

3 Layer Chili Dip

7 Layer Greek Dip

Boursin Ball

Deviled Eggs

Florida Salsa

Fried Oysters

Guacamole

Pastrami Ball

Stuffed Artichokes

Veal Spinach Loaf

3 Layer Chili Dip

Serves 4-6

My friend Sarah first introduced me to this dip in college. She made it during finals week one time and instead of studying we all just ate dip. Ahhh… college… when you can eat dip and a whole bag of chips and it doesn't really matter. If you are in a hurry, you can substitute canned chili for homemade and throw this together in a heartbeat.

Ingredients:
8 oz Cream Cheese, softened
1½ - 2 c Chili (pg. 36)
1 c shredded Colby Jack or Mozzarella Cheese

Preheat oven to 350
Spread the cream cheese evenly in the bottom of an 8x8 casserole dish.
Top the cream cheese with an even layer of chili.
Sprinkle the shredded cheese on top of the chili.

Bake, uncovered for about 30 minutes or until the cheese bubbles.

Serve with tortilla chips and/or Fritos.

7 Layer Greek Dip

Serves 8

I first had a version of this at my friend Amie's house. I kept asking for the recipe and she just told me to look it up on the internet. So I did. Then I changed it to suit my tastes, mostly by making my own tzatziki. This is a great dip to have out at parties. It is light and fresh and always disappears quickly. I like to serve it with pita chips.

Ingredients:
10 oz container Hummus
1 c Tzatziki Sauce (recipe below)
¼ c diced Cucumber
¼ c quartered Grape Tomatoes
¼ c Kalamata Olives, chopped
¼ c Crumbled Feta
1 T minced Red Onion

Spread the hummus in an even layer on the bottom of your serving dish.
Next, spread an even layer of the tzatziki on top of that.
Sprinkle with cucumber, tomatoes, olives, feta and onions.

Keep chilled until ready to serve.

Tzatziki Sauce

Makes about 1½ cups

This is a great Greek Sauce. You can use it in Seven Layer Greek Dip, by itself as a dip for pita chips and/or veggies and serve it with lamb.

Ingredients:
½ English Cucumber or 2 Mini Cucumbers
Salt
7 oz container whole milk Greek Yogurt
½ clove of Garlic, minced
¼ c Feta Cheese, crumbled
1 tsp chopped Dill
Squeeze of fresh Lemon Juice (optional)

Using the large holes on a box grater, grate the cucumber;
place in a fine mesh strainer and sprinkle with salt.
Let the cucumber sit in the strainer for at least 10 minutes (this will help the cucumber release its liquid).
Using your hand, squeeze as much liquid as you can out of the cucumber.

In a mixing bowl, combine the yogurt, cucumber, garlic, feta, dill and lemon juice.
Stir until well combined.

Boursin Ball Serves 6-8

Aunt Kathleen

My mom makes this all the time... ALL THE TIME. So much so that until I asked my mom for the recipe I had no idea it was actually my A. Kath's creation. So, thank you A. Kath! This is a family staple. There is never a Babor party without some sort of cheese ball present. Even if you fly the cheese ball from St. Louis to Los Angeles for your Oscar Party at the Beverly Hilton (this really happened)!

Ingredients:

8 oz brick Cream Cheese, softened
¼ c Butter, softened
½ tsp Beaumonde
1 clove Garlic, minced
1 tsp Water
1 tsp minced Parsley (plus extra for rolling at the end)
¼ tsp Red Wine Vinegar
¼ tsp Worcestershire Sauce
Pinch of: Sage, Savory, Rosemary, Thyme, Pepper (all dried herbs but if you have fresh, by all means use it) (plus extra pepper to roll at the end)

With electric hand mixer, beat softened cream cheese and butter until fluffy.
Add all remaining ingredients and mix.
Chill at least 1 hour (up to overnight).
When firm, shape into a ball or log.
Roll in parsley and cracked pepper; return to fridge until ready to serve.
Serve with crackers or flatbread.

Tips from my mom:

-Make a larger batch (she starts with 3 lbs of cream cheese); make several cheese balls and freeze, then roll in parsley and cracked pepper after thawed.

-Let it sit out 15 minutes before serving so softer and more flavorful.

Deviled Eggs

Serves 12

Ava

Everyone in the family makes deviled eggs, but my little cousin Ava loves them and makes them all the time. She has been making them for herself since she was 8. It makes me so happy when kids love to cook! These are Ava's deviled eggs and they are delicious!

Ingredients:

12 Eggs
2/3 c Mayonnaise
¼ c Yellow Mustard
1 T Pickle Juice
¼ tsp Salt
1/8 tsp Pepper
Paprika or Fresh Chopped Parsley (for garnish)

Hard boil (pg. 21) the eggs and peel.
Slice the eggs in half.
Remove all the yolks and place them in a bowl.
Mash the yolks with a fork.
Add the mayo, mustard, pickle juice, salt and pepper.
Continue to combine with the fork until smooth.
Spoon or pipe into the eggs.
Garnish with a sprinkle of paprika or parsley.

Florida Salsa

Serves A Crowd

JoEllen's Mom's Friend, Martha

This is my best friend's (Meribeth), friend's (JoEllen), mom's (JoEllen's mom), friend's (Martha) recipe. Are you following? So not exactly family but I have been making it for several years and my family members love it! It is so delicious and so easy.

Ingredients:

15½ - 24 oz jar of Salsa (I use mild, chunky salsa)
15½ oz can of Black Beans, drained and rinsed
15½ oz can of Corn, drained
4 sprigs of Cilantro, chopped
3 Green Onions, chopped
1 T Olive Oil
1 T Balsamic Vinegar
1 T Worcestershire Sauce
Few drops of Red Wine Vinegar
Few drops of Tabasco
2 tsp Garlic Powder
Juice of 1 Lime
Salt and Pepper

Mix all ingredients together.
Serve with tortilla chips and/or Fritos.

Drop the mic!

Fried Oysters

Serves 6

Dad

These were a staple in our house. Dad would make them sporadically but most often for Monday Night Football which was a big deal in our house. Especially if the Steelers were playing! It is just a shame I didn't like oysters at all until my late 20's. I missed out on decades of decadence!

Ingredients:
1 T Butter
1 T Olive Oil
1 c Milk
1/3 c Flour
2 Eggs
¾ c Breadcrumbs (pg. 108)
¼ c Flour
¼ c finely crushed Saltine Crackers (about 7 crackers)
1 lb Shucked Oysters

Prepare a frying pan over medium to medium-high heat with equal parts of butter and olive oil. *You need enough to coat the bottom of the pan; these are not deep-fried.*

Prepare your stations:
Remove oysters from container or shell and let the oyster liquid drip off as much as possible.
Place oysters in a bowl and pour in milk.
Put 1/3 c flour in a shallow bowl and mix in a little salt and pepper.
In another bowl, beat the eggs.
In the final bowl, combine the breadcrumbs, ¼ c flour and crushed saltines; stir until well blended.

Remove oysters from milk bath and dredge in the flour.
Shake off excess flour and dip in the beaten egg.
Let the excess egg drain off and dredge in the breadcrumb mixture.

Fry in prepared pan; about 3 minutes per side for a medium sized oyster.
Sprinkle with salt and serve with toast points.

Guacamole

Serves 6-8

I like very simple guacamole that tastes a lot like avocados. I also don't like spicy food. You can add more spice to this, of course, but don't loose the avocado flavor. Serve with tortilla chips or just eat it with a spoon like I do. It's healthier that way, right?

Ingredients:

3 Extra Large Haas Avocados
zest of 1 Lime
2 T freshly squeezed Lime Juice, divided
½ tsp Salt
¼ tsp Pepper
2 cloves Garlic, finely minced
1/3 c diced Tomatoes (seeded and very small dice)
1½ T Red Onion, finely minced
A couple dashes of Tabasco sauce

Drop the avocado halves into a mixing bowl and use a butter knife to cut into smaller chunks.
Add the lime zest, 1 tablespoon of lime juice and the next 6 ingredients.
Again, use the knife to cut or "mix" all the ingredients together.

(You can also use a fork if the knife seems difficult. You want all the ingredients evenly distributed but do not over mix, as you will mix again later.)

You can make the guacamole ahead of time and store in the fridge for a couple of hours.
To keep it from turning brown, pour the remaining tablespoon of lime juice on top of the guacamole and cover with plastic wrap.

When ready to serve, give the guacamole a final mix and spoon into serving dish.

Pastrami Ball

Serves A Crowd

Aunt Julie

We just can't seem to get enough meats and cheeses in this family. So of course we all love this, which combines the two! You can make one big cheese ball or 2 smaller ones (the "smaller" version is still the size of a softball). Grab a box of crackers and go to town.

Ingredients:

24 oz (3 bricks) Philadelphia Cream Cheese, softened (A. Julie says it has to be name brand)
3 oz Pastrami, shredded
3 oz Pastrami, very thinly sliced but not falling apart
1 bunch Scallions
3 T Worcestershire Sauce
¾ tsp Granulated Garlic Powder
½ tsp Salt

Using a handheld mixer, blend the cream cheese just until smooth.
Separate the shredded pastrami, or "fluff," then add to bowl.
Very thinly slice the white and light green parts of scallions; separate and add to bowl.
Using a spatula, mix all the ingredients together until they are evenly distributed and the mixture is smooth.
Taste and adjust seasonings as necessary.

Form the cheese mixture into a ball.
Lay out a couple of slices of whole pastrami slices, slightly overlapping.
Place cheese ball on top of pastrami slices, pull up the ends to "wrap" around the cheese ball.
Use the remaining slices to completely cover the sphere.
Wrap the cheese ball in plastic wrap and refrigerate for 24 hours.

Stuffed Artichokes Serves 2-3
Aunt May

These remind me of hanging out by the pool at A. May's house. They were always there to snack on. I now know how lucky I have been! Use them as an appetizer or part of the meal. Either way, they will be a hit!

Ingredients:
1 Artichoke
¼ - ½ c Breadcrumbs (pg. 108)
Dash Garlic Powder
Olive Oil
Pat of Butter

Rinse the artichoke.
Cut the bottom off the artichoke so it can sit.
Cut the top off of the artichoke and the pointy tip off of each leaf.
Fill each leaf with some breadcrumbs; I start from the outside (or bottom) and work my way in.
I try to stuff as many breadcrumbs in as I can but you can put in however much you want.
Sprinkle garlic powder over the artichoke.
Drizzle olive oil on top.
Put a pat of butter in the middle of the artichoke.
Steam them in a covered pot on the stove until you can pull the leaves out easily; about 1 hour.

Veal Spinach Loaf

Serves A Crowd

Aunt Marjorie

To me, this is my Aunt Marjories's signature dish. It is present at all of her fabulous Oscar Parties. It is so unique and delicious. Give it a try. Plus, it needs to be done 3 hours before your party. Always great to have something that doesn't need to be cooked at the last minute! You can serve this hot for dinner and it is delicious. The mustard sauce is seriously amazing. Make meatloaf sandwiches. It is in this section because we usually eat it cold as an appetizer but it really is very versatile!

Ingredients:
2 T Extra Virgin Olive Oil
1 medium Onion, minced
1½ tsp Dried Rosemary
1½ tsp Salt
½ tsp Pepper
10 oz pkg Frozen Spinach, thawed
1½ lb Ground Veal
½ lb Ground Beef
¾ cup seasoned dried Breadcrumbs (store bought)
2 Eggs, beaten

Mustard Sauce:
1 c Mayo
¼ c Dijon Mustard
2 T Worcestershire Sauce
1 T fresh Lemon Juice

Preheat oven to 350

Heat oil in skillet and cook onion, rosemary, salt and pepper until onion is tender.
Squeeze all of the water out of the spinach.
In large bowl mix spinach, onion mixture, ground veal and beef, breadcrumbs and eggs until well blended.

Line a loaf pan with plastic wrap (leaving a lot of overhang).
Firmly press all of the mixture into the loaf pan.
Invert loaf pan into the center of a 9x13 pan and let meatloaf slide out; remove all plastic wrap.
Bake for 75 minutes.

Meanwhile, mix all the ingredients for the mustard sauce in a small bowl until well blended; refrigerate until ready to serve.

When meat is done, place on platter, cover and refrigerate for at least 3 hours.
Cut into slices and serve cold with mustard sauce on the side, some crackers and/or baguette slices.

Sides

Baked Beans

Serves 14

Mom

These beans are excellent. In general, baked beans aren't necessarily my favorite but whenever these are around everyone gobbles them up! The only downside is that you have to make a pretty large amount; great for a barbecue with friends, not so great for a family of four. But, you can always freeze the leftovers in perfect family size portions for another night (or another 4 nights).

Ingredients:
½ lb Ground Beef
½ lb Bacon, chopped
1 medium Onion, chopped
15 oz can Kidney Beans, don't drain
15 oz can Butter Beans, don't drain
24 oz can Pork & Beans, don't drain
½ c Sugar
½ c Brown Sugar
¼ c Catsup
¼ c Barbecue Sauce
2 T Mustard
1 T Molasses
½ tsp Chili Powder
1 tsp Salt
½ tsp Pepper

Preheat oven to 350

In a large Dutch oven over medium high heat, brown the beef then remove it from the pot.
Drain the fat (from the beef and the Dutch oven).
In the same pot, add the bacon and cook until almost done.
Take out all but 1-2 tablespoons of the bacon grease; add the onions to the pot and sauté.

Once the onions are sautéed, add all the remaining ingredients to the Dutch oven.
Put the beef back in the pot.
Stir everything to combine.

Put pot in the oven, uncovered.
Cook for at least 1 hour, stirring occasionally.
The longer you cook them, the thicker they will get.

Creamed Spinach

Serves 6-8

This is one of my favorite side dishes ever! I have always been a fan of spinach, even as a child. But, creamed spinach is an extra special treat. I used to order it anytime we went out for a "steak dinner." Now, I can make it at home whenever I want and it is always just the way I like it! This recipe rivals any steakhouse!

Ingredients:
4 T Butter (½ a stick)
¼ of a small Onion, minced
2 cloves Garlic, minced
2 T flour
½ c Half & Half (optional)
1 c Milk (or 1½ c if not using Half & Half)
1 tsp Kosher Salt
¼ tsp Pepper
scant ¼ tsp nutmeg
2- 10 oz packages frozen Chopped Spinach, thawed and all the liquid squeezed out

Melt the butter in a large pan over medium heat.
Add onions and sauté for 5 minutes, stirring occasionally with a wooden spoon.
Add garlic and stir constantly for 30 seconds.
Add the flour and stir for 3 minutes; you should have a smooth consistency, no lumps.
Slowly pour in the half & half and/or milk while stirring constantly.
Add the salt, pepper and nutmeg; stir.
Continue to stir as the milk thickens.

After it has begun to thicken (about 3-5 minutes) add the spinach.
Stir everything together until it is well combined.
Leave on the heat, stirring occasionally, until the spinach is warmed through; about 7-10 minutes.
If the cream has gotten too thick, you can stir in some more (warmed) milk until you have your desired consistency.

Creamy Broiled Tomatoes

Serves 8

Mom

She didn't want to give me this recipe at first, but only for like a second. That's how good these tomatoes are. My mom makes them with big, beautiful summer tomatoes and they are fantastic. You can make about 8 large tomato halves. I like to make them with roma tomatoes so I make about 16 smaller halves. Enjoy!

Ingredients:

1 c Mayo
1 c grated Parmesan Cheese
¼ c Italian Seasoning
1 tsp Dried Basil
1 tsp Dried Rosemary
½ tsp Garlic Powder
½ tsp Salt
¼ tsp Pepper
4 large Tomatoes or 8 Roma Tomatoes

Mix first 8 ingredients together.
Cut tomatoes in half and place them cut side up on a baking sheet.
**Tip: Make sure the tomatoes can stand on the baking sheet; you can slice a small sliver off of the bottom of each half so they will sit flat.*
Spoon 2T of the mayo mix on top of each tomato and place directly under broiler.
Broil until they begin to brown and bubble; about 3 minutes.
You will have to watch them to make sure they don't burn!

Grandma's Green Beans & Potatoes

Serves 8-12

Aunt May

Okay, as the title implies, this was originally my Grandma Inchiostro's concoction but A. May gave me the recipe. She also made a huge batch for my high school graduation party. Thanks A. May! This is one of my favorite side dishes. It is so versatile and goes with so many main courses, especially with any kind of beef.

Ingredients:

1 lb Small Red Potatoes, whole
1 lb fresh Green Beans, trimmed
2-3 T Extra-Virgin Olive Oil
2 cloves Garlic, sliced or minced
Salt and Pepper
1-2 T chopped Parsley

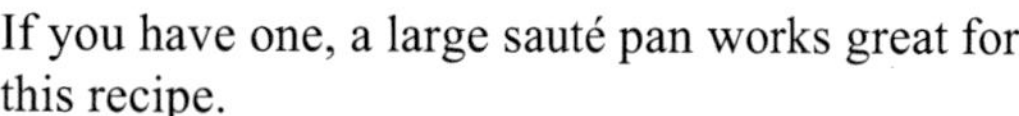

If you have one, a large sauté pan works great for this recipe.

Boil potatoes until a fork pierces them easily; about 10 minutes (depending on size of your potatoes).
Remove potatoes from the boiling water and set aside.
Add the green beans to the potato water and cook until just done, still with a little bite; about 5 – 7 minutes.
Drain green beans.

Meanwhile, quarter the potatoes.

Heat olive oil in the same pan over medium heat.
Add garlic and stir for 30 seconds.
Put green beans and quartered potatoes back in pot.
Season with salt and pepper.
Sprinkle with parsley.
Gently toss all to combine.
Serve warm or at room temperature.

Gravy

Serves 4-6

This gravy recipe has evolved over time to become the deliciousness that is listed below. I must admit… I'm quite proud of this one. My husband both loves and hates when I make it because he wants to eat it like soup. You don't have to include the mushrooms but I highly recommend it as it greatly enhances the flavor. But, if you want to leave them out just increase the butter by 1 tablespoon. Enjoy!

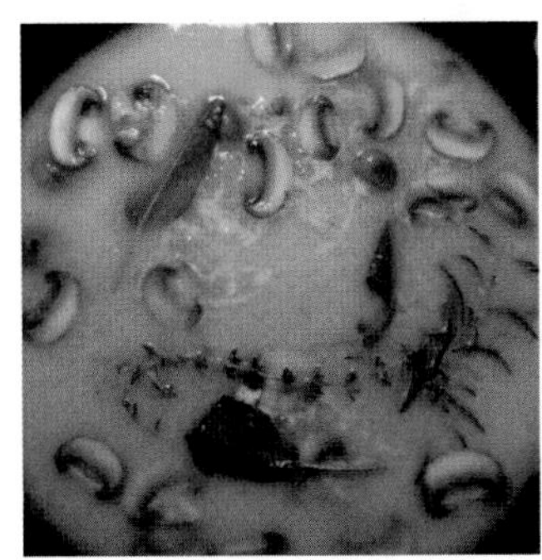

Ingredients:
8 oz Mushrooms, sautéed (pg. 78)
2 T Butter
3 T Flour
2 c Drippings and/or low-sodium Stock
(chicken, pork, turkey, etc.)
2 sprigs Thyme
4-6 leaves Sage
1 small sprig Rosemary
Salt & Pepper to taste
1 pat of Butter (optional)
1½ T Parsley, chopped

Sauté the mushrooms in a large sauté pan.
Once they are sautéed, add the butter to the pan and let it melt.
Add the flour and cook for 2-3 minutes while stirring constantly.
You want to cook out the raw flour taste (this is your "roux" or base for your gravy).
Slowly whisk in the warm drippings and/or stock.
Add the thyme, sage and rosemary and let the gravy simmer, stirring occasionally until it has reached your desired consistency.

Taste, adjust seasonings if necessary.
If you want, stir in an extra pat of butter to give your gravy a little shine.
Remove the thyme and rosemary sprigs and the sage leaves.
Sprinkle with fresh parsley and serve warm.

Hash Brown Casserole

Serves 12

Aunt Marjorie

I love potatoes and this hash brown casserole is just another delicious, cheesy way for me to eat them. They make a fantastic side dish; equally perfect for a brunch or barbecue. Enjoy!

Ingredients:

2 lbs frozen Hash Brown Potatoes, thawed
½ cup chopped Onion
1 tsp Salt
¼ tsp Pepper
10½ oz can Cream of Chicken Soup
1 pint Sour Cream
2 cups Shredded Cheddar Cheese
2 cups crushed Corn Flakes
¼ cup melted Butter

Preheat oven to 375
Combine first 7 ingredients in large mixing bowl.
Pour in a 13x9x2 dish sprayed with non-stick cooking spray.
Combine Corn Flakes with the melted butter and sprinkle over the top of the casserole.
Bake until browned and bubbly, about 45 minutes.
Let rest for 5 minutes and then serve it while it's hot!

Macaroni & Cheese

Serves 6

Influenced by Aunt Joy

It is amazing to me how often Macaroni & Cheese shows up at a family function now. I think there are so many great-grandchildren now that the aunts just figure "at least the kids will always eat this." Why wasn't that an option when I was growing up? No matter, I make up for it now at Christmas, Easter and the annual Pool Party.

Ingredients:
1/3 – ½ box of Macaroni noodles (or Shells)
3 T Butter
2 T Flour
½ tsp Salt
Dash of Pepper
2 c Milk (preferably warmed)
Dash of Nutmeg
8 oz Velveeta, cubed

Preheat oven to 350
Cook noodles in boiling, salted water until 2-3 minutes less than al dente (time should be on package).
Drain and rinse in cold water (an instruction almost never given).

Put the saucepan back on the stove and melt the butter over medium-high heat.
Add the flour and continue to cook while stirring for 1-2 minutes; add salt and pepper.
Add the milk while stirring constantly until well combined.
Add a dash or two of nutmeg.
Continue to stir and heat the milk until thick and bubbly.
**Tip- make sure you are scraping the sides and bottom of the pot while you stir. If anything burns the whole batch will be ruined.*

Add the Velveeta to the milk and stir until smooth.
Then, pour the noodles into the cheese sauce and stir to combine.

Spray a casserole dish with non-stick cooking spray and pour in the Mac n' Cheese.
**Make Ahead Tip- You can put it in the fridge at this point and cook it later if you want.*

Bake in a preheated oven for 30-40 minutes until it gets a little brown and bubbly.
Let sit for at least 5 minutes before serving.

Potato Salad

Serves 8

Aunt Joy

Aunt Joy's original recipe started with a 5 lb bag of medium red potatoes. That is what you will need for a large gathering. I halved her original recipe because I feel this amount is better for most occasions. Neither my husband nor I are huge potato salad fans but we can't seem to get enough of this!

Ingredients:

2½ lbs Red Potatoes
¼ Yellow Onion, minced
1½ tsp Salt
¾ tsp Pepper
1 c Hellman's Mayonnaise
(A. Joy says it has to be Hellman's)
1 T Yellow Mustard
2½ Stalks Celery, small dice
2 Hard-Boiled Eggs, diced (pg. 21)
Parsley, Green Onions or Chives, optional (for garnish)

Cover the potatoes (skin and everything) in cold water; bring to a boil.
Approximately 10-15 minutes after they have come to a rolling boil, stick a paring knife into the potato to see if they are done.
(If it goes through easily they are done, if not, cook a little longer and test again.)
Set potatoes aside to cool.
Put onions in a small microwaveable bowl, heat on high for 30 seconds.
Stir onions and set aside to cool.

Once cool enough to handle, peel potatoes and cut into bite sized pieces; add to large mixing bowl.
Sprinkle with salt and pepper.
Add all remaining ingredients and stir until well mixed.

Transfer to serving bowl and garnish with parsley, green onions or chives if desired.

Roasted Vegetables

Serves 4-6

This is my favorite way to eat any vegetable. If you aren't sure whether or not you like a vegetable, try roasting it. I would wager if you don't like it roasted, you won't like it any other way either.

This is most definitely a method and not a recipe. I use it for all types of vegetables: asparagus, broccoli, cauliflower, eggplant, parsnips, potatoes, radishes, turnips, etc... Always use the olive oil, salt and pepper but you will find what else you like as you go. Some examples: I only like brussel sprouts if they are shaved and roasted until they are practically burned. Carrots are excellent with a little dill sprinkled over them. Add some parmesan cheese to zucchini, brown sugar to sweet potatoes and cinnamon to acorn squash; all game changers. The possibilities are endless!

Ingredients:
1 lb Vegetables
1 T Olive Oil
½ tsp Salt
¼ tsp Pepper

Preheat oven to 425
Line a baking sheet with aluminum foil.
Place veggies on sheet pan, drizzle with olive oil and sprinkle with salt and pepper.
Using clean hands, toss everything together until evenly coated.
Place in oven and roast until desired doneness.

I recommend only putting one vegetable on a sheet pan. You can absolutely cook multiple veggies in the same oven but all of them cook for a different amount of time. By putting them on separate sheet pans you have more control.

Rough timing estimates:
Asparagus- roast 5-10 minutes depending on thickness.
Zucchini Rounds- roast 10-15 minutes depending on thickness; turn halfway through.
Broccoli Florets- roast 15-20 minutes, tossing halfway through.
Whole Carrots- roast 20-30 minutes depending on size, turning halfway through.

Sautéed Mushrooms

Serves 2-4

I never liked mushrooms until I was in my mid to late 20's. Now I eat them all the time but I usually use Portabella or Crimini (Baby Bella) mushrooms. I just like how "meaty" they are. These sautéed mushrooms are a great side dish on their own. But, even if you are going to add mushrooms as an ingredient to any dish, it really adds a great depth of flavor if you sauté them like this first.

Ingredients:
1 T Butter
1 T Olive Oil
8 oz Crimini Mushrooms
Salt & Pepper

You can leave your mushrooms whole, quarter them, slice them… whatever you want. Just try to make sure they are all roughly the same size so they cook evenly.

Heat butter and olive oil in a large sauté pan over medium-high heat (you don't want the mushrooms "crowded" in the pan).
When hot, add the mushrooms and a little salt and pepper.
Stir constantly so they will brown evenly.
The mushrooms will soak up the butter and olive oil; this is supposed to happen.
After a few minutes of constant tossing, they will start releasing the liquid back into the pan.

When browned to your liking, they are done.

Sides on the Grill

I love being able to make an entire meal on the grill, especially in summer when you don't want to heat up the whole house. My Dad is the master of the grill. Here are some recipes from him (and a couple from me) for sides that can be cooked on the grill. Whether you want a starch or a vegetable, we've got you covered. These all go great with any protein, from seafood to beef. Enjoy!

Corn on the Cob

Dad

Soak corn (in the husk) in water for at least 15 minutes.
Put corn (still in husk) on the grill.
Cook for about 15-20 minutes over medium heat, turning occasionally.
Peel back husk and silk and serve.
*Be very careful when husking, corn is HOT!!
This corn on the cob is AMAZING!

Herbed Veggies

Chop desired veggies into equal sizes (recommend Eggplant, Zucchini, Squash, Onion, Crimini Mushrooms).
**They will shrink a lot so don't cut them too small.*
Put all veggies in a bowl, drizzle with a couple of tablespoons of olive oil and sprinkle with salt, pepper and at least 1 Tablespoon of Herbes de Provence.
Stir to combine and evenly coat all veggies.
Pour veggies on grill grid or in veggie grilling basket over medium high heat, stir often.
Grill for about 20 minutes or until desired doneness.
Serve hot or at room temperature.

Potatoes (Serves 4-6)

2 large Russet/Idaho Potatoes, large dice
1 Vidalia Onion, large dice
6 cloves garlic, smashed
2 strips of uncooked bacon, sliced into lardons
1 T Extra Virgin Olive Oil
2 tsp Salt
1 tsp Pepper
1 T Butter

On a large baking sheet, lay 1 large sheet of heavy-duty foil perpendicular to the baking sheet.
Lay a second large sheet (twice as long as the baking sheet) of heavy-duty foil on top of the baking sheet; lightly spray that top sheet with nonstick cooking spray.
Place potatoes, onion, garlic and bacon on prepared baking sheet; drizzle with olive oil and sprinkle with salt and pepper.
Toss everything together with your hands so everything looks evenly coated/distributed.
Spread potatoes out so they are in one even layer.
Dot the butter evenly over the potatoes mixture.

Seal up the foil completely giving yourself a "handle" to grab.
Place foil directly on a hot grill. *(I only use the baking sheet to make it easier to carry; it does not go on the grill)*
Grill for about 20 minutes, shaking the foil pouch every so often to "stir" the potatoes.

Remove from grill.
Be careful opening the foil packet as there will be A LOT of steam.
Place in a dish and serve.
Fantastic! Especially the super crispy potato bits!

Teriyaki Vegetables

Dad

Slice the desired vegetables big enough so they can't fall through the grill (recommend Zucchini, Squash, Onions, Mushrooms).
Soak in teriyaki, salt and pepper for about 20 minutes.
Cook on the grill over medium high heat, turning once until desired tenderness, about 20 minutes.

Teeny Tiny Potatoes: 2 Ways

Serves 4-6

I LOVE Trader Joe's Teeny Tiny Potatoes. They are smaller than fingerlings and you can really just pop them in your mouth. They are very versatile and you just rinse them off to clean them. Easy! Below are two of my favorite ways to prepare them. Of course, you can use other types of potatoes in the recipes below and they will still be delicious. There is just something about those "Teeny Tiny" potatoes that I just can't get enough of.

Boiled

Ingredients:
1 lb Trader Joe's Teeny Tiny Potatoes
Olive Oil
1 T chopped Parsley
Salt
Pepper

Rinse potatoes in colander.
Put potatoes in medium pot and fill with cold water, cover with water by at least one inch.
Bring water and potatoes to a boil.
Heavily salt water when it starts to boil.
Boil potatoes until they are fork tender, about 10 minutes; drain.
Return potatoes to the hot pot.
Drizzle with olive oil, parsley, salt & pepper; toss to combine.
Enjoy warm or at room temperature (which makes them great for a party).

Roasted

Ingredients:
1 lb Trader Joe's Teeny Tiny Potatoes
1 T Olive Oil
scant ½ tsp Salt
¼ tsp Pepper
1 tsp Garlic Powder or Spice Blend (ex.- Herbs de Provence, Italian Seasoning or Cavender's All Purpose Greek Seasoning)

Preheat oven to 425

Rinse the potatoes in a colander.
Put potatoes in a pot and cover by at least one inch with cold water.
As soon as the water begins to boil, drain the potatoes.
Lay them on a kitchen towel until they are cool enough to handle.
**You can leave the boiled potatoes on the towel for a few hours if you want to do this step ahead of time. Boiling the potatoes first will give them a creamy texture on the inside.*
Slice each potato in half lengthwise and put on a baking sheet.
Drizzle with olive oil; sprinkle with salt, pepper and garlic powder/spice blend.
Toss everything together until evenly coated.
Roast potatoes in the oven for about 15-20 minutes tossing halfway through.
They will be brown and crispy on the outside and creamy on the inside.

Main Courses

Andy's Salmon with Brown Sugar Glaze

Serves 8

I never used to like salmon at all. It is a very strong flavor; you either like it or you don't. But I always keep trying things because, as your parents start telling you when you are two years old, "you might like it this time." So, I went to my cousin's house and they served this salmon. I was nervous because I hate salmon but I couldn't be rude so... I ate it. It was delicious!!! Now I like salmon every which way. I especially love this recipe and it turns out Every. Single. Time.

Ingredients:
1 T Brown Sugar
1 tsp Honey
1 T Butter
2 T Dijon Mustard
1 T Soy Sauce
1 T Olive Oil
1 tsp dried Ginger
1 whole Salmon fillet, skin on (about 2.5 lbs and 1" thick)

In a small saucepan over medium heat, melt the brown sugar with the honey and butter.
Remove from heat and whisk in the mustard, soy sauce, olive oil and ginger.
Allow to cool.

Place the salmon, skin side down, on a large sheet of foil. Trim the foil to leave a ½ inch border around the edge of the salmon.
Coat the salmon with the brown sugar mixture.

Grill the salmon indirectly over medium heat until the edges begin to brown and the inside is opaque, 25-30 minutes.
Turn off the heat and serve fish directly from the grill.

-or-

Carefully transfer the salmon with the foil to a large cutting board.
Cut the salmon crosswise into 8 pieces, but do not cut through the skin
Serve pieces directly from cutting board by sliding a spatula between the skin and flesh. The skin will stick to the foil so it works really well.
Serve immediately.

Baked Chicken Breasts

Serves 4

This is probably one of the first recipes I ever "created" by myself. It is simple, quick and delicious. Chicken breasts can be so boring but not with a little bit of Italian flair. Mangia! Mangia!

Ingredients:
4 boneless, skinless Chicken Breasts
½ - 2/3 c Wishbone Italian Dressing
1½ c Breadcrumbs (pg. 108)

Preheat the oven to 350

Put the chicken breasts in a Ziploc bag.
Pour over the dressing; squeeze the air out of the bag and seal.
Let sit on counter for about 15 minutes.

Line a baking sheet with a piece of foil then put an oven safe cooling rack on top.
Put breadcrumbs in a pie plate or flat bowl.
Take out one chicken breast at a time, letting the dressing drain off a bit.
Dredge the chicken in the breadcrumbs so it is completely coated and place on prepared baking sheet.
Repeat with remaining chicken breasts.
Bake until cooked through, about 25-30 minutes (assuming 6-8oz breasts).
Let stand for 5 minutes, then serve warm.

Baked Ham

Feeds A Large Crowd

Mom

Ham is a Babor family staple. There is always a GIANT ham at major holidays. Always bone –in and never spiral sliced. We get the real deal. And even though ham freezes great I don't need a whole ham when baking one just for my family. I buy half a ham and always the butt portion (not the shank). I do that because my mom told me to and the woman knows her ham! This recipe is for the whole thing, but I did the math for you if you are only making half below.

Ingredients:
22-24 lb Bone-In Ham
Whole Cloves
2/3 c Brown Sugar
¼ c Honey
4 tsp Mustard
Heavy splash Orange Juice

Preheat oven to 250
Place ham in a large roasting pan.
Use a knife to score a criss-cross pattern in the top of the ham; cutting 1/8 – ¼ inch down.
Place cloves in each "x" you cut on the top of the ham.
In a mixing bowl, stir the brown sugar, honey, mustard and orange juice together until you have a relatively smooth paste.
Smear the sugar mixture all over the top of the ham.

Put the ham in the oven.
Baste the ham every 45 – 60 minutes using the drippings from the pan.
Bake for 4-5 hours.
**The ham is already fully cooked, you are really just warming it.*

Remove from the oven and let someone else carve it for you!

Butt Portion Modifications:
1/3 c Brown Sugar
1/8 c Honey
2 tsp Mustard
Splash of Orange Juice

Prepare the same way.
While baking, put a piece of foil on the cut end of the ham to help prevent it from drying out.
Bake at 200 for 3 hours, basting every 45 minutes.

Barbecued Chicken

Serves 4-6

Dad

My dad is known for cooking "forever." On the weekends if we ate by 10pm we felt lucky... and he had started cooking at 2. I don't know how this happened or how his food was never dry or burned. He is the master of the slow cook. I do not have the time or patience for that, as I am ALWAYS hungry! Here is dad's delicious flavor with my sped up time frame. Unlike most other things I grill, chicken does need to cook a little slower because no one wants "rare chicken" ... otherwise known as food poisoning and salmonella. Follow these steps and you will get delicious chicken every time. Feel free to mess with the measurements; this is just a starting point.

Ingredients:

1 Whole Cut Up Chicken (or 5-6 lbs of your favorites pieces)
3 T Olive Oil
2 tsp Salt
1 tsp Pepper
1½ tsp Garlic Powder
Your favorite BBQ Sauce

Put all the pieces of chicken in a large mixing bowl.
Drizzle with olive oil and season with salt, pepper and garlic powder.
Take a large wooden spoon and "stir" it all up; make sure all chicken is evenly coated with the oil and seasonings.

Have a medium hot grill ready to go.

Put the chicken pieces on the grill according to size.
**If you have a giant chicken breast it is going to take longer to cook than a little leg, so put the breast on first. I always use bone in, skin on pieces. You don't have to but cooking times will be shorter for boneless, skinless pieces.*

Put the chicken on skin side down.
Do not move them until the skin gets a little crispy; about 7 minutes.
Then, turn the chicken over and continue to cook another 7 minutes.

If your chicken is cooking too quickly, turn down the grill.
**Chicken is the one thing I will flip a few times since I am trying to cook it all the way through. It may stick to the grill a little but since you put olive oil on, it shouldn't be too bad.*

Continue cooking for another 5 – 10 minutes or so depending on the piece of chicken, flipping a couple more times.
**Don't worry about the chicken being all the way cooked through at this point. Make sure it looks delicious on the outside. Nice and grilled with brown, crispy skin.*

Line a large baking sheet with foil and place an oven safe cooling rack on top.
Remove all the chicken and put onto your prepared baking sheet.
No, I did not forget about the BBQ sauce. We are not going to sauce it on the grill.
Sauce On Grill = Big Old Mess!

Pour some BBQ sauce into a bowl and get out your basting brush.
Brush the sauce onto each piece of chicken.
I usually sauce the "underneath" first, then flip it over and sauce the skin-side.
After all the chicken has a light coating of sauce, place the baking sheet in the oven.
**I like a lot of sauce but I know I shouldn't assume everyone does. You can serve with extra sauce on the side.*

Turn the oven on to 200 degrees and let sit in there for at least 20 minutes.
The sauce will stick to the chicken and if anything is under-cooked, it will finish cooking in the low oven.

Beef Tenderloin Serves 8-10

Aunt Clare and Aunt May

I LOVE beef tenderloin. It is one of the very easiest things in the world to make and there is almost nothing more delicious and impressive to eat. It does have one downfall- it's expensive. That is why we usually save beef tenderloin for special occasions. You don't always have to buy a whole one; sometimes I will ask the butcher for a one-pound piece if we are treating just ourselves. But for our purposes here I will tell you how I prepare a whole (already trimmed) beef tenderloin. I have recipes from both my A. Clare and my A. May. After making them for years this is what I do and it works every time...

Ingredients:
5 lb trimmed Beef Tenderloin
Kitchen Bouquet
Salt
Pepper
Garlic Powder
Snider's Seasoning

There are no measurements; this is all done to your personal taste. Just remember, this is a very big piece of meat so sprinkle on a little more seasoning than you think is necessary. Warning- this is a messy job. There is no other way to prepare this than to get your hands dirty.

Get your grill hot!

If you have "skinny" end, fold it up and tie with kitchen string so the tenderloin is as close to even thickness all the way through as you can get it.
Rub Kitchen Bouquet all over the tenderloin.
Season all over with salt, pepper, garlic powder and Snider's Seasoning *(you can do this the night before if you want to).*

On the grill, sear the tenderloin on all sides; about 3-4 minutes per side.
Wrap the tenderloin completely in foil until you are ready to roast *(you can sear the meat up to 2 hours before you put it in the oven, just leave it on the counter until you're ready).*

Preheat the oven to 500

Put a very large piece of foil on a baking sheet; put the seared tenderloin on the foil.
Roast in the oven for 16 minutes for rare to medium-rare.
If you like your meat a little more done, leave it in a little longer but probably not more than 20 minutes.
Take it out of the oven and use the large piece of foil under the roast to wrap it up. Leave the tenderloin to rest for 10-15 minutes.
Move the roast to a cutting board with a well, slice and arrange on a serving platter.
Pour some of the juice from the foil or cutting board over the sliced meat.

Boeuf Bourguignon

Serves 8

This sounds like a fancy dish but it is really just beef stew; a traditional French, delicious, beef stew. And I mean fantastically delicious! It is a dish that simmers for hours and fills your home with comfort. It tastes great after sitting in the fridge for a day and it freezes beautifully. Goes perfectly with a French Burgundy, of course, and some crusty bread for soaking up all the juices.

Ingredients:
1 T Olive Oil
¼ lb Bacon, cut into lardons
3 lbs Boneless Short Ribs
3 cloves Garlic, minced
1 T Tomato Paste
1 bottle Dry Red Wine
1 c Beef Stock
2 large sprigs Thyme
6 large Carrots, cut diagonally into 1-inch thick slices
½ lb frozen Pearl Onions
2 T room temperature Butter
2 T Flour
¾ lb Crimini Mushrooms, quartered
Parlsey, chopped (for garnish)

Put a large Dutch oven on the stove over medium-high heat.
Drizzle 1 tablespoon of olive oil in the pot and cook the bacon, stirring often, until crispy.
While bacon is cooking, season the short ribs with salt and pepper on both sides.
Remove the bacon with a slotted spoon, drain on a paper towel and set aside.

Brown the short ribs, on all sides, in the bacon fat.
Do not crowd the pan, brown in 2-3 batches if necessary.
Remove meat and set aside in a bowl.

Discard some of the fat, leaving only 2 tablespoons in the Dutch oven.
Add the garlic and cook for 30 seconds, stirring constantly.
Add the tomato paste and brown for 30 seconds while stirring constantly.
Pour in the wine and deglaze the pan for 1-2 minutes, scraping the brown bits off the bottom of the pan.
Add the beef stock, thyme, and a little salt and pepper; stir.
Bring to a boil; reduce to simmer and cook uncovered for 10 minutes.

If you want, you can cut the short ribs into smaller, bite sized pieces (Personally, I like everything in big chunks for this dish).
Return the meat with all its juices to the pot.
Simmer, covered for 2 hours; stirring every once in a while.
After 2 hours, remove the thyme sprig stems.
Add carrots and lowly simmer with lid on a tilt for another 40 minutes; stir occasionally.
Add onions and simmer for an additional 20 minutes (still keeping the lid on a tilt).

Meanwhile, sauté the mushrooms separately (pg. 78).

With a fork, mash the butter and flour into a paste; gently stir into the sauce.
Simmer for 2 minutes to thicken.

Add mushrooms and their juice to the pot.
Add the bacon back in.
Stir everything to combine and… Voila, Boeuf Bourguignon!

You can eat the stew just like that or serve it over boiled potatoes or egg noodles. My personal favorite though is to serve over mashed potatoes. Garnish with parsley and enjoy!

Brian's Lamb Lollipops

Serves 4

Let me start by saying I have never liked lamb. I have tried it in super fancy restaurants that know how to cook it and I still have never liked it. One day our friends were having a pool party and my friend Brian brought these over. I didn't want to eat one because a) I don't like lamb and b) lamb is expensive so I wouldn't want to waste an entire chop. Under pressure, I took a bite of my husband's just to try it. I'm telling you they were AMAZING! I still won't order lamb in a restaurant and would be hesitant to try it anywhere else but I could eat these all day, every day. Many thanks to Mr. Condon for being so generous and sharing his fantastic recipe.

Ingredients:
2¼ - 2½ lbs French Cut Lamb Chops
3 T Olive Oil
2 Cloves Garlic, minced (about 1 T)
1½ T (or more) Cavender's All Purpose Greek Seasoning

If necessary, cut rack into individual chops.
Drizzle half of olive oil over lamb and massage onto lamb so it is nicely coated.
Sprinkle ½ of garlic and ½ of the Cavender's over the lamb and rub in.
Flip chops and repeat with remaining oil, garlic and Cavender's.
Cover and let marinade in fridge for at least 3 hours.

Prepare grill for medium heat.

Usually I like meat cooked rare to medium rare and I think that would be the recommended temperature for lamb. However, the first time we had this they were medium and I really liked them that way so that is how we cook them.

The thickness of a lamb chop can vary greatly which means cooking times will vary greatly.
For thin chops, cook them about 3½ - 4 minutes per side and go up from there.

When your chops are done, put them on a platter and let them rest for 10 minutes, then DEVOUR!

Chicken Pot Pie

Serves 4-6

We LOVE pot pie in this family! We even had a pot pie throw down for Christmas one year... I lost to my sister Angie, but I have upped my game since then so don't worry! One of pot pie's greatest attributes is versatility. I have certain vegetables and pie crust listed in the recipe below but you can add any leftover vegetables you have in the fridge. And I have also topped with puff pastry and biscuits. I don't even know what my favorite is because they are all fabulous. Enjoy!

Ingredients:
4 T Butter, divided
1 small Onion, chopped
2 stalks Celery, chopped
3 Carrots, chopped
Salt & Pepper
1 small Potato, small dice
2 tsp Olive Oil
1 tsp Herbes de Provence (optional)
¼ tsp Garlic Powder
3 T Flour
2 c Low Sodium Chicken Stock (plus extra if necessary)
½ tsp Poultry Seasoning
1 T fresh Parsley, chopped
½ c Frozen Peas
½ c Frozen Corn
2 c cooked Chicken, cubed
2 Pie Crusts

Preheat oven to 400
In a deep skillet, melt 2 T butter over medium heat.
Add onions, celery and carrots; season with salt and pepper.
Sweat/sauté veggies, stirring occasionally until softened; about 10 minutes.

Meanwhile, toss diced potatoes on a small baking sheet with the olive oil, Herbes de Provence, garlic powder and a little more salt and pepper.
Roast in oven for 7 minutes, toss and roast for an additional 5 minutes; set aside.

Add remaining 2 T of butter to the onion mixture and let it melt completely.
Add the flour to the pan; cook for 3 minutes while stirring to cook out the raw flour taste.
Slowly add the chicken stock, while stirring continuously, until you have smooth sauce.
Season with poultry seasoning, parsley and a little more salt and pepper.
Let simmer for 3 minutes.
Add potatoes, peas, corn and chicken; stir everything together.
Taste and adjust seasonings as necessary.

Line a pie plate with the first piecrust.
Fill with pot pie mixture and press down to remove air bubbles.
Place second pie crust on top, trim edges and seal (the easiest way is with a fork).
Cut a few vents in the top of the pie crust.
Place on a cookie sheet and bake in the preheated oven until browned and flaky, about 45 minutes.

Let rest at least 10 minutes before serving.

Justin's Fish

Serves 6

My friend Justin is not necessarily known for his cooking- more for his good looks and winning charm. But he hosted a potluck brunch one Sunday and this was one of the dishes he made. It was AMAZING. Every time I make it I wonder why I don't make it more often. I even like the leftovers and who likes reheated fish? Thanks Justin!

Ingredients:

20 oz bag refrigerated Shredded Hash Browns (usually in the dairy section of the grocery store)
4 cloves Garlic, minced
1 tsp Salt
5 T Extra-Virgin Olive Oil, divided
½ c pitted Spanish Green Olives, roughly chopped
15 oz can of Fire Roasted Diced Tomatoes
¼ cup diced Roasted Red Peppers
2 Scallions, chopped
2 T chopped Parsley
1½ lbs skinless Tilapia filets (about 3 filets)
1 tsp Herbes de Provence
Salt & Pepper

Preheat oven to 425
In a bowl, toss the hash browns, garlic and salt.
Heat 2 tablespoons of olive oil in a large nonstick ovenproof skillet over medium to medium-high heat.
Add the hash browns and press down with a spatula; cook until the bottom is golden brown, about 12 minutes.

Slide the hash browns out of the pan and onto a plate, keeping in one piece.
Drizzle 2 tablespoons olive oil into the pan and let heat for a minute.
Quickly flip the potato cake off of the plate into the hot pan.

Flip the plate away from your body! Oil will splash and you don't want it to splash on you!

Again, use spatula to smash down the hash browns.
Cook until crisp and golden, about 10 minutes.

Meanwhile, mix the olives, tomatoes, roasted peppers, scallions and parsley in a bowl.
Cut the fish into equal sized pieces. *(I usually double the "thin" half of the tilapia filet to make one piece and cut the "thick" half of the filet into two pieces. If using 3 filets, I end up with 9 pieces total).*

Season each piece of fish (on both sides) with the herbs, salt and pepper.

Scatter half of the olive mixture over the potato cake and top with the fish.
Scatter the remaining olive mixture on top of the fish and drizzle with the remaining tablespoon of olive oil.
Transfer the skillet to the oven and bake until the fish is cooked through, about 12 minutes.

Lemon Chicken on the Grill

Dad

I remember having this all the time as a kid. We would play in the backyard while dad was at the grill for (at least) 4 hours. We would run over to the grill and get 1 bite of chicken every ½ hour or so. Now it's my turn to let the kids play in the backyard while I sip a drink and slowly grill and baste my chicken (but I cut down the 4 hours). A great summertime, weekend meal! The olive oil to lemon juice ratio changes with every family member you ask. Dad's is heavy on the oil but I prefer heavy on the lemon juice. Play with the ratios until you find your favorite.

Ingredients:

Chicken (your favorite pieces... Thighs!)
1/3 c Olive oil, plus extra for drizzling
2/3 c freshly squeezed Lemon Juice
1 T dried Oregano
3 cloves Garlic, minced
Salt and pepper
Celery stalk with leaves or Parsley stalks (optional)

In large bowl drizzle a little olive oil over all chicken pieces and sprinkle with salt and pepper. Mix well so everything is evenly coated.

Whisk together 1/3 cup of olive oil, lemon juice, oregano, garlic, salt and pepper in at least a 2 cup measuring cup.
It will separate again; just stir it up a little every time you are going to use it.

Cook chicken over indirect heat on the grill.
Using the celery stalk as your brush, brush the lemon mixture on the chicken.

Continue to cook over indirect heat for about an hour, turning and marinating often; if fire is too hot it will burn the outside and not cook the inside.

So Good! Enjoy!

Oven Roasted Brisket

Serves 8

Aunt Carol

Aunt Carol told me how she makes her brisket over lunch one day. I don't even remember how we started talking about it but she was the first one to tell me to put French Onion Soup Mix on brisket and roast it slowly in the oven. I took it and ran with it. So, so good. If you are roasting anything over 4 ½ lbs consider using 2 packets of French Onion Soup Mix (but don't double the wine) and a disposable foil pan instead of a baking sheet and aluminum foil.

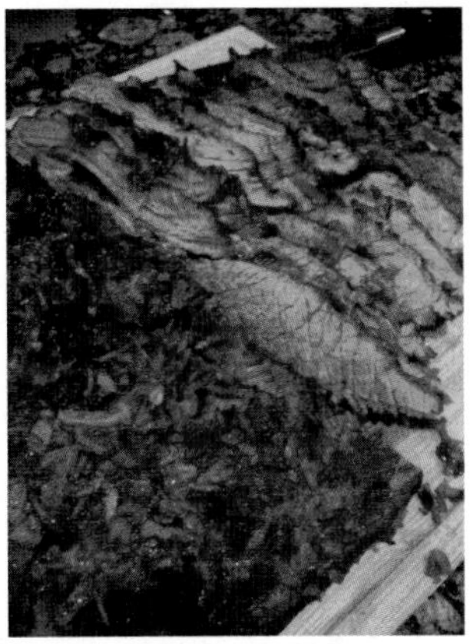

Ingredients:
4 lb Beef Brisket
1 packet French Onion Soup Mix
1/3 c dry Red Wine

Preheat the oven to 250

Trim some of the excess fat off the top of the brisket, but not all.
Place a large sheet (or two) of heavy-duty foil on top of a baking sheet.
Put the brisket, fat side up, on top of the foil.
Sprinkle the top of the brisket all over with the entire packet of soup mix.
Pour the wine onto the foil around the brisket.

Seal up the foil so the brisket it completely enclosed (without the foil touching the brisket on the top or sides).
Roast for at least 4 hours (or about 1 hour per pound) until the brisket is tender.
Let rest for 15-30 minutes before slicing.

**Make a day ahead. Don't slice the brisket and put it in the fridge. Then next day you can scrape the fat off of the top before slicing and reheating.*

Ratatouille

Serves 6

Let me be completely honest... I watched the Disney/Pixar movie Ratatouille and was inspired. I didn't even have kids at the time but that truly is how this recipe came about. I started looking up different recipes online and mixed and matched things. I kept tweaking it every time I made it until I settled on the recipe below. I'm certain this is not the traditional French peasant dish but more like Ratatouille: Italian style. This is a great vegetarian main course. It is a lot of steps but it is delicious! You can prepare the whole dish ahead of time and keep it in the fridge until you are ready to bake. Enjoy!

Ingredients:
3 T Olive Oil, plus some extra
2 large Eggplant, cut into ½ inch cubes
4-5 cloves Garlic, minced
1-2 T chopped Parsley
1 large Onion, sliced into half moons
1 Zucchini, thinly sliced into rounds
2 cups sliced Portabella Mushrooms
3-4 Roma Tomatoes, sliced
1 c grated Parmesan Cheese, divided
Salt and Pepper to taste

Preheat oven to 350
Spray bottom and sides of a 1½ quart casserole or an 8x8 dish with nonstick cooking spray

Heat olive oil in pan over medium high heat.
Add eggplant to pan, sprinkle with salt and pepper and sauté for about 10 minutes or until soft.
**I often leave the lid on a tilt while doing this or I find I have to keep adding olive oil. The eggplant will really shrink down after it is cooked through.*
Add garlic and parsley to the pan; stir for another 20-30 seconds.
Spread eggplant mixture evenly across bottom of prepared casserole dish.
Sprinkle with a few tablespoons of Parmesan cheese.

Add a little more olive oil to the pan; add onions.
Season onions with salt and pepper and sauté for 5-10 minutes.
As the onions are cooking, place zucchini slices on top of the eggplant in the casserole dish.
Sprinkle zucchini lightly with salt, pepper and some more cheese.
Place sautéed onions on top of the zucchini and sprinkle with cheese.

Continue layering in this fashion with the uncooked mushrooms and tomatoes, covering each layer with a light sprinkling of salt, pepper and cheese.
Bake in preheated oven for 45 minutes.

As it bakes, a delicious vegetable broth will form.
Excellent served over Acini de Pepe noodles to soak up all that broth (especially if the noodles are cooked in chicken stock but then it's no longer a vegetarian dish).

Ribs

Serves 2-4

Dad

I'm assuming you are far enough into this cookbook that you now know my dad enjoys the slow grilling process. I tried to speed up the time on these and you just can't. You have to cook ribs slow and low so you can get that fall off the bone tenderness. Enjoy!

Ingredients:

1 slab of Pork Spare Ribs
Olive Oil
Garlic Powder
Salt
Pepper
Onion Powder
Paprika
Cayenne Pepper
1½ oz Beer
1½ oz Water
BBQ sauce (optional)

Lightly drizzle both sides of the slab with olive oil.
Sprinkle both sides with your desired amount of each of the spices. *(I go a little heavy on the garlic powder, of course, and extremely light on the cayenne pepper).*

Cook indirectly for "a long time" (I think dad said you can cook them "forever"), at least 1 ½ -2 hours.
Mix the beer and water together.
Carefully put ribs in heavy foil and pour the beer/water mixture over the ribs.
Wrap the foil up totally so the steam doesn't escape.
Cook indirectly for at least another 30 minutes (or longer, again… "forever")
If desired, you can put barbecue sauce on at the table.

**If you do want BBQ sauce that is a little "sticky" on the ribs, follow the same method as described in the Barbecued Chicken recipe (pg. 86).*

Roasted Pork Loin

Serves 6

I feel like pork gets a bad wrap. People think it can be dry; it can be... if you over cook it. Roast this just until the internal temperature hits 135 and let it rest for at least 10 minutes. If you do that it will come out perfectly every time. This roasted pork is simple, not at all dry and absolutely delicious. Pour some gravy over it (pg. 73)... even better!

Ingredients:
2½ – 3 lb Pork Loin
2 large Carrots
Large sprig of Thyme
Small sprig of Rosemary
6 large Sage leaves
Olive Oil
Salt
Pepper
Garlic Powder

Preheat oven to 450
Peel carrots and lay in a baking dish.
Put the herbs in between the carrots.

Rinse the roast and pat dry.
Drizzle the pork with olive oil and rub all over.
Then, sprinkle all over with salt, pepper and garlic powder to taste.

Place pork, fat side up, on top of carrots (the carrots act as a rack).
Roast in the oven at 450 for 15 minutes; reduce heat to 300 and cook another 40 minutes or until the internal temperature reaches 135.

Remove from oven and cover with a piece of foil; let rest for 10 minutes (the pork will continue to cook as it rests).
Slice and serve warm.

Short Rib Pot Pie

Serves 4-6

Comfort Food. That's all I have to say!

Ingredients:

2 T Olive Oil, divided
1 lb boneless Short Ribs
Salt & Pepper
1 c diced Potato
2-3 T Butter (if necessary)
1 small Onion, diced
3-4 Carrots, diced
2 stalks Celery, diced
2 cloves Garlic, minced
3 T flour
1 T Tomato Paste
2 c low-sodium Beef Stock (warmed if possible)
Splash of Dry Sherry (optional)
1 large sprig Thyme
1 Bay Leaf
4 oz Baby Bella Mushrooms, quartered and sautéed (pg. 78)
2 Pie Crusts

Preheat oven to 425
In large deep skillet/sauté pan drizzle 1 tablespoon of olive oil and turn heat to medium-high.
Season short ribs with salt and pepper on both sides.
Brown in the hot pan until there is a good brown "crust" on the meat on all sides; about 15 minutes total.
Remove from pan and set aside.

While the meat is browning, put your potatoes on a sheet pan.
Drizzle with the remaining tablespoon of olive oil and season with salt and pepper.
Toss everything together until evenly coated (if you want to add some herbs here too that would be delicious).
Roast potatoes in oven for 10 minutes (tossing halfway thru).
Remove from oven and set aside.

After you have set the meat aside, you need 3 tablespoons of fat in the pan.
Either remove all but 3 tablespoons of the fat from the pan, or, if the short ribs didn't produce enough on their own, add the necessary amount of butter.

Reduce heat to medium.
Add onions, carrots and celery to the pan; season with salt and pepper.
Cook veggies gently in the pan, stirring often, about 7-10 minutes or until softened.
Add garlic and cook for another minute, stirring constantly.
Add flour; cook for 3 minutes while stirring often to cook out the raw flour taste.
Add tomato paste and brown the tomato paste for 1-2 minutes.
Add the beef stock while stirring constantly until you have a smooth consistency.
Add splash of sherry if using.
Adjust the temperature as necessary to make sure the stock is at a simmer.
Add the thyme and bay leaf; continue to stir often.
Add the mushrooms and any collected juices to the pan.

Cut the short ribs into bite-sized pieces; add back to the pan along with any collected juices; simmer at least 10 minutes.
Taste and adjust seasoning if necessary.
Add the potatoes.
Stir everything together.

Meanwhile, roll out one piecrust and put in pie plate.
Remove the thyme stem and the bay leaf from mixture then pour into pie plate.
Top with the second crust and crimp the edges with your fingers or a fork.
Cut vents in the top crust.
Cover the edges of the crust with a pie shield or aluminum foil to prevent burning.

I highly recommend putting your pot pie on a foil-lined baking sheet before putting in the oven (to protect from overflow).

Bake pot pie for about 50 minutes or until the crust is nice and brown.
Let rest for at least 15 minutes before cutting.
Enjoy!

**Make Ahead- You can prepare the pot pie earlier in the day. Keep it covered in the fridge and bake it before dinner.*

Short Ribs

Serves 8

I love short ribs. I use them in stews and soups but in this dish the short ribs are the star. Enjoy!

Ingredients:
4 lbs Short Ribs
2 T Butter
3 stalks Celery, chopped
2-3 Carrots, peeled and chopped
1 medium Onion, chopped
3 T Tomato Paste
1 ¼ c dry Red Wine, such as Chianti
½ c Medium Dry Sherry
½ c low-sodium Beef Stock
3 cloves Garlic, peeled
2 Bay Leaves
2 sprigs Thyme

Sprinkle short ribs on both sides with salt and pepper.
Melt butter in a Dutch oven or very large sauté pan (with high sides) over medium-high heat.
Brown short ribs on all sides, working in batches if necessary, until browned; about 10 - 15 minutes per batch.
**Make sure not to crowd the pan or they won't brown properly.*
After browned, remove short ribs from pan and set aside.

Remove all but 2 tablespoons of fat from the pan.
Add celery, carrots and onion to pan.
Sprinkle with salt and pepper and sauté until onions begin to soften and brown, stirring often; about 5 minutes.
Add tomato paste and brown for about 1-2 minutes, stirring often.

Add wine and sherry to the pan.
Simmer for two minutes while scraping up any browned bits off the bottom of the pan.
Add stock, garlic, bay leaves and thyme; stir together and continue to simmer.

Return ribs to the pan along with any juices that have collected; arrange them in a single layer.
(You can prop them on their sides if necessary).
Cover, reduce heat to medium low, and simmer 1½ hours.
Occasionally move ribs around to prevent them from sticking to the pot.

Using tongs, turn ribs over in pot.
Cover and simmer for another 1½ - 2 hours, stirring occasionally, until short ribs are very tender.

Then, simmer uncovered to thicken the sauce; about 20 minutes or until sauce has reached desired consistency.
Remove thyme sprigs, bay leaves and garlic cloves.
Serve warm over creamy polenta and spoon some of the sauce on top.

**Make a day ahead and put it in the fridge. The next day, scrape the fat off of the top before reheating on the stove.*

Stuffed Red Peppers

Serves 4-8

I've been experimenting with this recipe since I read The Bridges of Madison County. They make vegetarian stuffed peppers in that book. I mentioned this to my mom all those years (decades) ago and she said she makes them with white rice and ground beef. Neither of those versions sounded good to me. So, I came up with this. It doesn't look like much when you just have one pepper sitting on a plate for dinner but I can never even finish it. It is a whole meal in a pretty package. If you want a smaller version, slice the peppers in half and fill each half as opposed to the entire thing. Then it would feed 8 instead of 4 and you could add a salad or some roasted veggies on the side. These would also be very easy to serve at a dinner party or set up on a buffet. I love the versatility.

Ingredients:
4 Red Peppers
2 T Olive Oil
1 small Onion, chopped
3 cloves Garlic, minced
1 lb boneless, skinless Chicken
2½ c Hot Water
1 bag Vigo Saffron Yellow Rice
Parsley or Green Onions for garnish

Preheat oven to 350
Cut the top of the peppers (like you would a pumpkin) and take off the "lid" along with the seeds.
Remove any excess ribs as best you can.
Rinse out the inside of the peppers to remove any remaining seeds.
Make sure the peppers can stand; if necessary, slice the smallest bit from the bottom of the pepper so it can stand.
Put the peppers in a pot and cover with cold water; put the lid on and bring to a boil.
Once the water starts to boil, carefully remove the peppers from the pot with tongs, draining water out as you go.
Place peppers in baking dish sprayed with non-stick cooking spray.

Meanwhile, heat olive oil in large sauté pan with a tight fitting lid.
Cut chicken into small bite-sized pieces.
Sauté the chicken, stirring often for about 2 minutes.
Add the onion and cook for another 2 minutes.
Add garlic and cook for another 30 seconds.
Add the hot water and bring to boil.
When the water boils add the saffron rice.
Stir for 1 minute, reduce heat, cover and simmer for 20 minutes

**The rice mixture should be a little watery still. If it is not, add water by the ¼ cupful and stir.*

Stuff the peppers with the chicken and rice mixture, really pack it in.
Cover each pepper with at little square of foil. *(This will help keep the rice mixture from drying out).*
Place in the oven until the peppers are soft, about 15 minutes. Enjoy!

VARIATIONS:

-You could do a quicker version of this by just making the rice according to the package and adding cut up, store bought rotisserie chicken.

-You can add extra veg in by adding a small 10 oz package of frozen chopped broccoli into the rice mixture

-You can give it even more depth of flavor by cooking the rice in a mix of chicken stock and white wine and adding some extra saffron.

The Perfect Steak

This looks like a lot of instructions for what is really a very quick and simple recipe. It is really more of a method than a recipe; a method that will lead to the perfect steak every time. You will notice, there aren't any measurements. They all depend on both the size of your steak and your personal taste. Just go with sprinkling and drizzling and it will be great! Mangia! Mangia!

Ingredients:
Steak (I recommend Rib Eyes)
Extra-Virgin Olive Oil
Kosher Salt
Pepper
Garlic Powder

Pull your steak out of the fridge and let it come to room temperature.
Drizzle the steak with a bit of olive oil and rub it all over.
Season both sides with salt, pepper and garlic powder (I use a lot of garlic powder, I'm Italian).
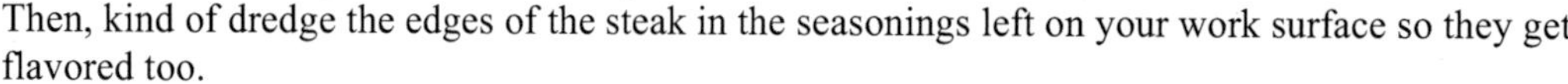
Then, kind of dredge the edges of the steak in the seasonings left on your work surface so they get flavored too.

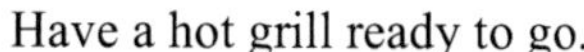
Have a hot grill ready to go.
Cooking times will depend on the thickness of your steak.
For a steak at least 1 inch thick, grill with the lid closed for about 4½ minutes per side.

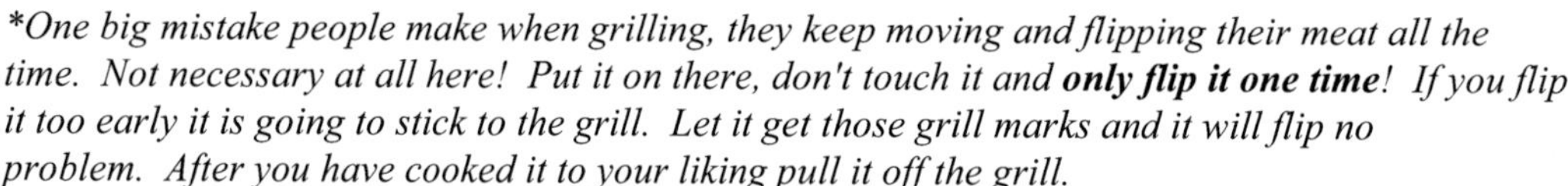
One big mistake people make when grilling, they keep moving and flipping their meat all the time. Not necessary at all here! Put it on there, don't touch it and **only flip it one time! If you flip it too early it is going to stick to the grill. Let it get those grill marks and it will flip no problem. After you have cooked it to your liking pull it off the grill.*

Most importantly LET YOUR MEAT REST!
Put it on a cutting board and cover it with a piece of foil.
Let it rest for about 10 minutes before serving or slicing.

Italian

Accidental Braciole Pasta

Breadcrumbs

Chicken Cacciatore

Lasagna

Lemon Caper Sauce

Linguine with Clam Sauce

Meatballs

Pasta Sauce

Pork Ragu

Salsiccia Casserole

Scaccia

Spedini

Zucchini Casserole

Accidental Braciole Pasta

Serves 8

As the name implies, this pasta was an accident. I was trying to make Braciole: a piece of beef stuffed, rolled and braised in pasta sauce. It was all going swimmingly until the end when I tried to slice the Braciole. Instead of nice slices of meat, it all just started shredding (I probably rolled it the wrong way or didn't slice against the grain). So, what was I to do but put the shredded meat back in the pot of sauce and serve over noodles. It was AMAZING. One of the best mistakes I have ever made!

Ingredients:
1½ lb Flank Steak
3 T Extra Virgin Olive Oil, divided
Salt & Pepper
¾ c Breadcrumbs (pg. 108)
1/3 c chopped Parsley
1/3 c shredded Italian Blend Cheese
1 c dry Red Wine, such as Chianti
1 batch of Pasta Sauce (pg. 115)
Basil (optional)

Lay flank steak on a work surface and pound out until it is an even thickness.
With 1 tablespoon of oil, lightly oil both sides of the flank steak.
Lay the steak out so the short end is closest to you.
Sprinkle with salt and pepper.
Then, sprinkle evenly with the breadcrumbs, leaving a 1" border on the sides and at the far end.
Drizzle the breadcrumbs with olive oil.
On top of breadcrumbs, evenly sprinkle the parsley and the cheese.

Carefully roll the steak, starting at the short end, trying to keep all of the filling enclosed.
Tie with kitchen twine to secure.
Sprinkle the outside of the braciole with salt & pepper.

In a large Dutch oven, heat 2 tablespoons of olive oil over medium-high.
Sear the braciole until it is nice and brown on all sides, about 2-3 minutes per side, 8-12 minutes total.
Carefully remove the braciole and set aside.

Pour the wine into the pot and scrape up all the brown bits on the bottom.
Let simmer for about 2 minutes.
Add the pasta sauce and stir until combined.
Turn the heat down to keep the sauce at a low simmer.

Put the braciole along with any juices that collected back into the pot.
Simmer, with the lid on, for at least four hours until the meat is very tender; seven hours would be better.
I turn and baste the meat every 30-45 minutes.
Remove the braciole.
Cut off the kitchen twine and start shredding the beef with two forks.
Don't worry about the filling spilling out.
Scrape everything, shredded meat and filling back into the sauce; stir to combine.
The sauce will thicken when you add the filling back in.
If desired, thin the sauce with pasta water.

I like to serve tossed with pappardelle noodles.
Garnish with ribbons of fresh basil (chiffonade).

Absolutely delicious!

**For a more traditional braciole, add some sliced hard-boiled eggs to the filling. Instead of shredding the beef, remove it and let it cool for about 20 minutes. Slice it into ½ inch thick slices. Toss the noodles with some sauce, lay the slices of braciole over the noodles and spoon some sauce over the braciole slices. Garnish with some fresh basil.*

Breadcrumbs
Aunt May

About 10 Cups

These are a staple ingredient! You must have them! As my father said, "They're like bacon; they make everything taste better." Making them is a bit of a process and they can be expensive too because of all the Parmigiano-Reggiano cheese. BUT it makes a ton of breadcrumbs and it is totally worth the effort. I promise! Just keep them in the freezer use them whenever you want. They will last forever and you will be so happy you have them. Sidebar- this is the recipe that when I asked A. May "how much" she yelled at me, "I don't know, until it smells right!"

Ingredients:
6 c day-old French or Italian bread (1 loaf)
2 c grated Parmesan cheese
1 c finely chopped fresh Parsley (1 bunch)
6-8 cloves Garlic, minced
Salt & Pepper

Cube bread then finely grind bread in a blender or food processor.
*(*No need to cut off the crust)*
Add cheese and parsley.
Add minced garlic.
Add salt and pepper to taste.
Stir everything together to combine.

Freeze breadcrumbs so they are always ready for use.

You will find your own ways to use these but here are some of the recipes just in this book alone that call for these breadcrumbs:

Fried Oysters (pg. 63)
Stuffed Artichokes (pg. 66)
Baked Chicken Breasts (pg. 84)
Accidental Braciole Pasta (pg. 106)
Meatballs (pg. 114)
Spedini (pg. 124)
Zucchini Casserole (pg. 125)

Chicken Cacciatore

Serves 4

Cousin Rose Mary

Rose Mary said they would always prepare this for the men for their annual deer hunt. It was easy for them to heat up in a cabin or eat at room temperature. I am just preparing it for my family for dinner, but I love to know everything I can about these family recipes!

This is really a recipe to experiment with, adding more or less of each ingredient until it is perfect for you. You can also double or triple it easily if wanting to serve it for a crowd! The original recipe called for bone-in Chicken Breasts, but boneless suits us just fine. Add about 20 minutes of cooking time if you use bone-in.
Sidebar- You can double just the sauce if you want a second meal the next night. The sauce is delicious and great over pasta. Mangia! Mangia!

Ingredients:
4 (5-6oz) boneless, skin-on Chicken Breasts
Salt & Pepper
Flour for coating
2 T Olive Oil
½ a small Onion, thinly sliced
2 clove Garlic, minced
15 oz can Tomato Puree
¼ c Red Wine
½ tsp Sugar (optional)
3 large Basil leaves, cut into ribbons (chiffonade); plus extra for garnish
1 T drained Capers
4 oz Mushrooms, quartered and sautéed (pg. 78)
heaping 1/3 c pitted Olives, halved (I like Castelvetrano)
Splash of Red Wine Vinegar

Season the chicken with a little salt and pepper.
Lightly coat the chicken breasts in flour, shaking off any excess.
Heat 2 tablespoons of olive oil in a large sauté pan or Dutch oven over medium-high heat.
Brown the chicken breasts on both sides until golden brown, starting with the skin side down (about 7 minutes per side).
Remove chicken and set aside.
Add onions to the pan; sprinkle with salt and pepper and sauté until translucent (about 5 minutes).
Add garlic and sauté for another minute, stirring constantly.
Add tomato puree, wine, sugar (if using) and basil.
Bring to a boil then reduce to a simmer.
Add capers and mushrooms; cook gently for 5 minutes.
Add olives and vinegar, stir to combine.
Nestle the chicken into the sauce and cook on medium low heat for about 20 minutes (otherwise the sauce will scorch).
Flip the chicken a couple times while cooking.
Alternatively, you can cover and bake at 300 in the oven for about 20 – 30 minutes.

You can serve directly from the Dutch oven. However, the ideal way is to arrange the chicken breasts in a deep platter and cover with generous amounts of sauce.

Lasagna

Serves 12

There is no way around it; lasagna is an involved process. It isn't hard, just a lot of steps. But of course it is all worth the effort! Especially when you consider it can feed you for days... and it seems to taste better after sitting for a day, doesn't it? Freeze part of it and have it again in a month or two!

Ingredients:
1 lb Lasagna Noodles
2 lbs Salsiccia, cooked and drained (Italian Sausage, I like mild)
1¼ lb Ricotta Cheese
4 oz Goat Cheese, at room temperature
1 T Olive Oil
2 eggs, beaten
1 c Parsley, chopped
1½ tsp Salt
¾ tsp Pepper
12-15 oz frozen Chopped Spinach, thawed and water squeezed out (optional)
1 batch of Pasta Sauce (pg. 115)
1 lb shredded Mozzarella Cheese
1 c Parmigiano Reggiano

Preheat oven to 325

Cook lasagna noodles in a pot of boiling, salted water for about 3-4 minutes.
Carefully drain the noodles and leave them in a pot/bowl of cold water (this will stop the cooking process and keep them from sticking together).
In a mixing bowl, combine the ricotta cheese, goat cheese, olive oil, eggs, parsley, salt and pepper with an electric hand mixer.

Spray your lasagna pan with non-stick cooking spray
Layer:

1. Sauce
2. Noodles
3. Sauce
4. Ricotta Mixture
5. Spinach
6. Salsiccia
7. Mozzarella
8. Parmesan

Repeat layers 2-7 and then finish off with a layer of:

1. Noodles
2. Sauce
3. Mozzarella
4. Parmesan

Bake for 20 minutes covered with foil then for an additional 20 minutes uncovered, or until cheese is brown and bubbly.
Let sit for 20 – 30 minutes before serving.

*You can assemble the lasagna the day before and keep it in the fridge. If you do, bake for 30 minutes covered and 30 minutes uncovered, or until cheese is brown and bubbly.

Lemon Caper Sauce

Aunt May

Serves 8-12

This Lemon Caper Sauce is delicious. Apparently my Aunt May came up with the recipe because she was starving waiting for a repair person and just threw together what she had laying around the kitchen. I don't know that my kitchen is always this well stocked but I'm glad hers is because now we can all enjoy this creation. This recipe originally was for pasta but really it's all about the sauce; it is so versatile. Put it on chicken, fish, steak... And the best part, the sauce freezes beautifully!

Ingredients:
1 T (at least) minced Garlic
1/3 c Olive Oil, divided
2/3 c White Wine (such as Pinot Grigio)
1½ sticks Butter
Zest of 1 large Lemon
1/3 c fresh Lemon Juice
1/3 c Capers
1 c chopped Parsley
3 c thinly sliced Mushrooms, sautéed (pg. 78)
¾ c chopped Basil
½ c Pine Nuts, toasted
Parmesan Cheese (optional) for serving

In a large sauté pan drizzle a little bit of the olive oil and sauté your garlic over medium-high heat. Once it has a good sizzle add the wine and let it simmer for a few minutes until it reduces by half. Add the remaining olive oil and the butter; stir together as the butter melts.
Add the lemon zest, lemon juice, capers and parsley; stir to combine.
Simmer for about 5 minutes.

Add mushrooms.
**You must sauté the mushrooms before adding them to the sauce or they will absorb all of the lemon flavor as opposed to enhance the sauce with their flavor.*
Simmer for about 3 minutes.

Add the basil and toasted pine nuts; stir to combine.
**To toast pine nuts put them in a dry pan over medium-high heat. You must stir them constantly and watch them. They can burn quickly.*

If putting the sauce over pasta, put a little sauce in the bottom of the serving bowl; add the hot pasta and toss together.
Add sauce as needed, you will most likely have leftover sauce (which is great because you can freeze it).
Serve with Parmesan cheese for sprinkling.

*This recipe can really be played with. Aunt May says she would use at least 4 cups of mushrooms (because she loves them). My cousin Catherine almost doubles the Pine Nuts (because she loves them). Wine was not in the original recipe but I added it (because I love it). So, this is definitely a recipe where you can "make it your own."

Linguine with Clam Sauce

Serves 6 -8

In general, I order things at restaurants that I don't or can't make at home. It is a good rule of thumb. This has always been one of my favorite dishes to order at an Italian restaurant, Linguine con Vongole. Then I discovered, I could make this at home. And it is actually very quick, easy and delicious.

Ingredients:
1 lb Linguine
¼ c Butter
¼ c Olive Oil
3 cloves Garlic, minced
2/3 c White Wine
2- 6.5 oz cans Clams (minced or chopped)
2 T chopped Parsley
2 T Shredded Basil
Salt & Pepper to taste

Put a big pot of water on and bring to a boil.
Heavily salt the boiling water and add the linguine.
Cook one minute less than Al Dente (should be on package).

As the noodles are boiling, heat the butter and olive oil over medium-high heat in another large pot.
Add the garlic and stir for about 30 seconds.
Add the wine; let simmer and reduce for a couple of minutes.
Toss in the clams with all of their juices, parsley, basil, salt & pepper.
Let the sauce continue at a low simmer while your noodles finish cooking.

Don't worry that the sauce is thin; the noodles will soak up the sauce.

When noodles are ready, use tongs to transfer them to the clam sauce.
Toss everything until well combined. If you need to, add a little pasta water.

Serve with a sprinkle of fresh parsley and/or basil and enjoy!

Meatballs

Serves 4-6

Grandma Inchiostro/Aunt May

These are one of those things where, what you grew up with is what you like. I have never ordered meatballs in a restaurant. I don't even know if I would order a meatball in Italy. These are our meatballs and they are the best! I don't know why everyone wants to drown their meatballs in sauce. Fry them and eat them just as they are in all their glory!

Ingredients:
Olive Oil for frying
1lb Ground Chuck
1½ c Breadcrumbs (pg. 108)
1 c Parsley, chopped
2 Eggs
¼ c Water
Salt & Pepper

Coat the bottom of a large pan with about ¼ inch of oil.
Turn to medium to medium-high heat.

In large bowl break up the meat.
*(*I usually use a serving fork for breaking up the meat and mixing as A. May taught me.)*
Add breadcrumbs and parsley to the bowl.
Break the eggs into the side of the bowl, tilt the bowl to the side a bit and beat the eggs a little.
Add water, salt and pepper.
Starting with the serving fork, mix everything together until ingredients are evenly distributed but don't over mix or the meatballs will be tough.

Roll the meatballs but again, don't work with the meat too long or they will get tough; just form them and carefully put them in the hot pan.

Fry in the hot pan until they get nice and crusty brown.
Continue to turn the meatballs until all sides are evenly browned.
Remove to a paper towel lined plate and immediately sprinkle with salt.

The Best Meatballs Ever!

**Making Ahead-*
If you are making meatballs for a crowd you do not want to be frying all of them while your guests are enjoying cocktails. Fry them early and either refrigerate or freeze them. To reheat (thaw if they are frozen), I line a baking sheet with parchment paper and put the meatballs in an even layer. Warm in a low oven (about 200 degrees) until heated through (at least 20-30 minutes).

**In Sauce (if you must)-*
Meatballs can add flavor to your pasta sauce. If you want to do this only fry them until very crispy on the outside. Don't worry about the inside being cooked all the way. They will continue cooking in the sauce. Only add them for the last 30 minutes of simmering and be careful when you stir, you don't want them to break up in the sauce.

Pasta Sauce

About 4-5 Cups

Grandma Inchiostro/Aunt May

This is our pasta sauce; it is very simple and that is how it should be. My A. May adds basil to the sauce, my Grandma did not, nor do I. I do however garnish pasta with fresh basil when it is served. As you will see, this sauce is used in a few dishes throughout the cookbook. But most importantly, this is the sauce for my ultimate comfort food: spaghetti and meatballs.
Mangia! Mangia!

Ingredients:
3 T Olive Oil
1 medium Onion, chopped
4 large cloves Garlic, minced
6 oz can of Tomato Paste
28 oz can San Marzano Crushed Tomatoes
Salt & pepper
½ c chopped Parsley (about 8 big stems)
½ c chopped Basil (optional)

Heat olive oil in large saucepot over medium heat.
Add onion to the pot, season with salt and pepper and sauté until soft and translucent, about 10 minutes, stirring often.
Add garlic and stir constantly for 30 seconds.
Add tomato paste and brown for 1 minute.
Add crushed tomatoes; season with salt and pepper.
Fill the can of tomato paste with water 3 times and add it to the pot.
If you are not using San Marzano tomatoes, add a dash of sugar.
Stir in parsley.
Reduce temperature and simmer up to 3 hours; stir every 10-15 minutes while scraping the bottom and the sides.
The longer you cook the sauce the thicker it will become.

If desired, add basil to sauce about 15 minutes before you are finished cooking.

Tips:
1. If you want you can add a few meatballs; they will help flavor the sauce. See the meatball recipe for more info on adding meatballs to pasta sauce.
2. Double or triple the batch and freeze it in serving sizes that meet your needs. It freezes beautifully and it isn't really any more difficult just a little more chopping and can opening.

Pork Ragu

Serves 8

When you hear the term "Sunday Sauce" this is what I think of. This is an all day sauce. It isn't difficult but it has a lot of steps and it cooks for a long time. It is a labor of love and it will show. Totally worth the effort!

Ingredients:
2 T Extra Virgin Olive Oil
1½ lb bone-in Pork Shoulder
Salt & Pepper
1 small to medium Onion, diced
3 medium Carrots, diced
3 stalks Celery, diced
5 cloves of Garlic, minced
6 oz can Tomato Paste
18 oz White Wine
28 oz can San Marzano Crushed Tomatoes
6 oz Water
1 c Parsley, chopped
1 sprig Rosemary
1 stem Sage
1 large sprig Thyme
3-4 oz Mascarpone Cheese

In large Dutch Oven, heat olive oil over medium-high heat.
Season pork shoulder with salt and pepper.
Sear until brown and crusty (about 7 min. per side); remove pork shoulder and set aside.

Meanwhile, put the onions, carrots and celery into a food processor and chop/grind until very fine (the mixture will almost resemble a paste).
Add the veggies to the Dutch oven, season with salt and pepper and brown the veggies for about 3-5 minutes, stirring often; add the minced garlic and stir for 30 more seconds.

Add the tomato paste and brown for about 1 minute, stirring constantly.
Fill the tomato paste can with the wine and add to pot, do this three times total.
Stir until well blended while scraping up all the brown bits on the bottom of the pot.
Turn the temperature down and continue to simmer for another minute.

Stir in the crushed tomatoes.
Fill the tomato paste can with water.
Use that water to "rinse" the crushed tomato can, then add to pot.
Add the parsley and a little salt and pepper.
Using a piece of kitchen twine, tie the rosemary, sage and thyme together (this is called a bouquet garni) and put in pot.
Put the pork shoulder back in along with any juices that have accumulated.
Give a little stir and let simmer for 2½ - 3 hours, stirring occasionally.

Remove the bouquet garni and discard.
Remove the pork shoulder and shred all the meat with two forks.
Throw away the bone then put the shredded pork back in the sauce; stir in mascarpone cheese.

Congratulations, you have just made an AMAZING sauce! Toss with 10 – 12 oz of pappardelle noodles and garnish with some chopped parsley.

Salsiccia Casserole

Serves A Crowd

Salsiccia is Italian sausage. It is pronounced Sa-Zeet-Za. I think I originally got this recipe from my cousin Ellie, who probably has her mom's (Aunt Clare's) version but I believe the original creator was Aunt May. And like a game of "Telephone" this is my version...

Ingredients:

1 pkg Wide Egg Noodles
2 T Butter
1 lb Salsiccia (I always use mild)
1 small-medium Yellow Onion, chopped
¾ cup sliced Black Olives
¼ cup chopped Parsley
1 tsp Salt
½ tsp Pepper
1 bag of Italian Blend Cheese, divided
1½ - 2 pints Grape Tomatoes, sliced in half, divided
Juice of ½ a Lemon
3 beaten Eggs

Preheat oven to 350
Spray a large casserole dish with nonstick cooking spray (a soufflé dish works great); set aside.
Cook noodles and drain.
Put back in pot and toss with butter.

Meanwhile, in a separate skillet, brown the salsiccia (if necessary remove casing first).
Add onion and cook until soft; about 5 minutes.

To the noodles add the salsiccia mixture, olives, parsley, salt & pepper, 1 big handful of the cheese and half of the tomatoes.
Pour the lemon juice over the mixture; stir all ingredients together.
Pour beaten eggs over mixture and toss.

Put ½ the noodle mixture in the prepared casserole dish and press down a little.
Sprinkle with ½ the remaining tomatoes and ½ of the remaining cheese.
Repeat the layers with the remaining ingredients.
Cover with foil and bake for 45 – 50 minutes until the cheese is nice and bubbly.

So unique and delicious!

Scaccia

Great Aunt Helen

This is one of those things that elicits wonderful memories. My Great Aunt Helen is my Grandpa Inchiostro's youngest sister. She is 100 years old and she is amazing! I mean the youngest 100 year old on the planet! We didn't see her all the time growing up, maybe 2-3 times per year but every time we did I was always hoping there would be scaccia (pronounced scotcha).... and there always was! She makes 3 different kinds but I was always partial to the broccoli. And by partial I mean it is the only one I ever ate. I didn't eat the other two until I started recipe testing and I must admit, they are fantastic too. I was missing out for all those years. I am so grateful she shared the recipe with me. She clearly goes big when she makes this as the dough recipe started with 12 cups of flour and the sauce started with almost 7 pounds of tomatoes. I have pared all that down here. Aunt Helen said it will take practice to get it right and you will figure it out as you go along. Try one at a time, make one of each, do whatever you want but I promise you will not be sorry!

Scaccia Dough

Makes 3 Scaccia Loaves

Ingredients:
1 pkg Dry Active Yeast
10 oz Warm Water (not hot)
1 tsp Sugar
3 c Flour
½ tsp Salt
1 tsp Olive Oil

Pour yeast, water and sugar into a bowl and let sit for about 5-10 minutes.
Add flour, salt and olive oil; stir everything together.
Put on floured board and kneed for ½ hour, adding flour as necessary.
Put in an oiled bowl, cover and let rise about 1 hour.
Punch down, cover and let rise again for another ½ hour.

Broccoli Filling Enough to fill 2 loaves

Ingredients:
2 heads Broccoli
¾ c Olive Oil
3-5 cloves Garlic, minced
pinch of Baking Soda
Salt & Pepper

Preheat oven to 375

Wash your broccoli and cut into pieces. *(Aunt Helen says to make sure it is REALLY dry. She lets it dry overnight.)*
In a large bowl combine broccoli, oil, garlic, baking soda, salt and pepper.
Stir all together and let marinate for about 1 hour (while making your dough and letting it rise).

Roll the dough into a circle.
Fill ½ of the dough with the broccoli filling and fold over.
Close up the ends by pinching, twisting or using a fork to seal.
Put on parchment lined baking sheet.
Cover with a towel and let rise for 15-20 minutes.
Cut 3 slits in the top.
Bake for 35 minutes or until golden brown.

Let cool for at least 15 minutes then slice into 1½" strips for serving.

Salsiccia & Ricotta Filling Enough to fill 2 loaves

Ingredients:
1 lb raw Salsiccia
1 lb Ricotta
1 T Olive Oil
Salt & Pepper
1-2 T Parmesan Cheese
1 Egg, slightly beaten

Preheat oven to 375

In a bowl, mix the ricotta, oil, salt, pepper, Parmesan and egg until well combined.

Roll out dough into a long rectangle.
Alternately dot large chunks of salsiccia and ricotta cheese all over the dough (so it looks like a checkerboard), leaving about a 1-inch border all around.
Fold over the dough as many times as necessary then, seal the edges with your fingers or a fork.
Place on a parchment lined baking sheet.
Cover with a towel and let rise for 10-15 minutes.
Make three slits in the top, going halfway through the dough.
Bake for 1 hour or until golden brown.

Let cool for at least 15 minutes then slice into 1½" strips for serving.

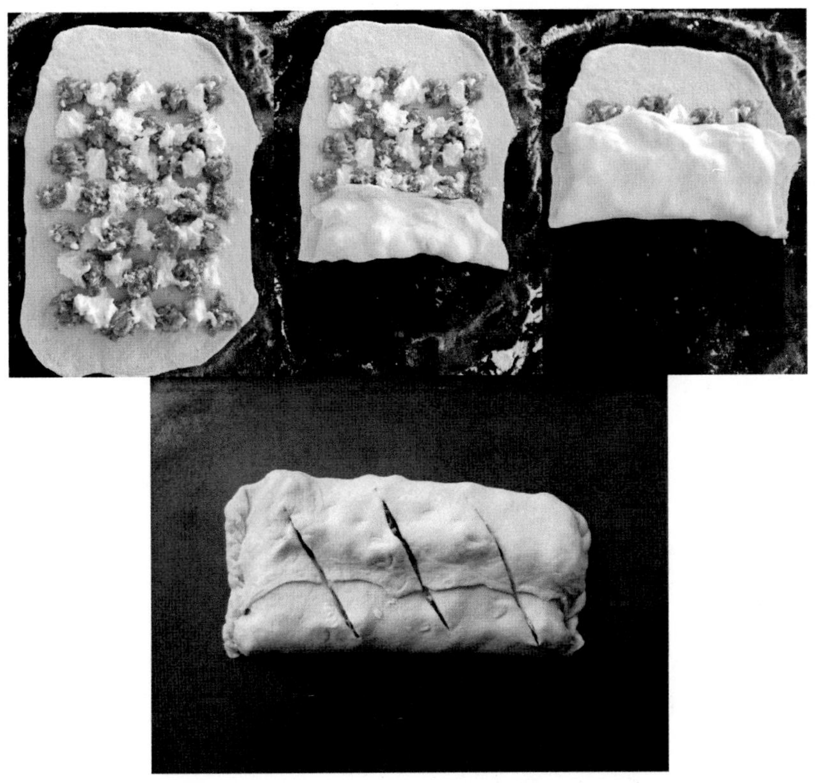

Cheese and Scaccia Sauce Filling Enough to fill 2 loaves

Ingredients:
1 c domestic Romano Cheese
1 c Scaccia Sauce (see below)

Preheat oven to 375

Cut the hunk of Romano cheese into thin chunks. **Aunt Helen said you should use domestic Romano; the imported is too strong and will "burn your face."*
Mix the chunks of cheese and sauce in a bowl together.
Roll the dough out into a long rectangle; roll out the dough thin!
Spread sauce all over the piece of dough leaving a 1-inch border all around.
Fold the dough over as many times as necessary then use your fingers or a fork to seal the ends.
Place on a parchment lined baking sheet.
Cover with a towel and let rise 10 minutes.
Prick all over with a large fork (a fork that is part of a carving set) and bake for 40 minutes, or until golden brown.

Slice into 1½" strips for serving.

Scaccia Sauce

This is a marinara sauce my Great Aunt Helen makes. She makes a ton of it and cans it. The recipe she gave me starts with almost 7 pounds of tomatoes! I'm going to pare that down and I do not plan to can it. This version is for immediate use for scaccia or you can use as a general marinara sauce. You can easily double, triple or quadruple if you want to can it. She always makes this in a large sauté pan, never a pot because "it needs air."

Ingredients:
28 oz can of Whole Tomatoes (A. Helen uses fresh but I'm taking the shortcut)
½ head Garlic, peeled and minced
1½ T Olive Oil (A. Helen does not use Extra-Virgin, just regular olive oil)
1 tsp Sugar
½ tsp Salt
¼ tsp Pepper
Pinch of Baking Soda
1½ c Basil leaves- cleaned and dry

Pour tomatoes and all their juice into a bowl and squeeze with your (clean) hand to crush.
Use an immersion blender or put in a blender to chop, but don't chop too much.
In a large saucepan, sauté the garlic in the olive oil for about 1 minute over medium-high heat; make sure the garlic doesn't burn.
Add the tomatoes to the saucepan.
Add the sugar, stir and let simmer.
While simmering and thickening add the salt, pepper and baking soda.
Continue to simmer.
After simmering for about an hour total, taste and adjust seasonings (sugar, salt and pepper) only if necessary.

Turn off the heat.
She really stressed that you need a lot of basil; if you need more than 1½ cups of basil, make sure you have it available.
Chop or use your kitchen shears to cut the basil; add to saucepan and stir to combine.

*Specifically when using for scaccia- add another teaspoon of olive oil to the sauce right before you are making your scaccia.

Spedini

Serves 16 as an app, 8 as main dish

Mom and Dad

I have been told that "spedini" in Italian means "skewered meat." For this reason, spedini is completely different from one place to the next. These are my family's spedini and they are to me, of course, the best! Kind of like meatballs, I won't even try them at a restaurant. My parents both make them. Over a decade ago I asked each of them for their recipe. My mom sent me hers on half a sheet of paper and my dad sent me two full pages. Funnily enough, they are essentially the same. I have tried to combine them and this is what I ended up with...

Ingredients:

2 lbs Top Round- ask your butcher to slice them scaloppini style
1 medium Onion, small dice
1½ - 2 large Tomatoes, small dice
3 cloves Garlic, minced
1 c Extra Virgin Olive Oil
4 c Breadcrumbs (pg. 108)

Preheat broiler
Line a baking sheet with foil and top with an oven safe cooling rack.

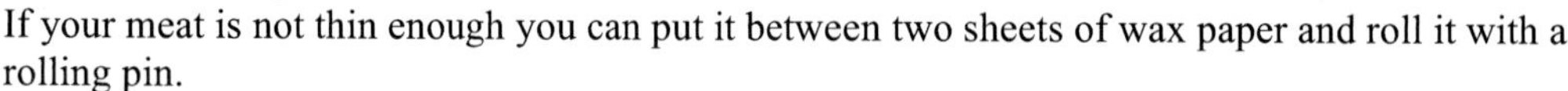

If your meat is not thin enough you can put it between two sheets of wax paper and roll it with a rolling pin.

Soften the onions in the microwave for 1 minute, stirring halfway through; let cool.
Seed tomatoes and dice.
In a bowl mix together the tomatoes, onions and garlic.

Set up your stations (pie plates work well):
1 bowl with olive oil
1 bowl with breadcrumbs
1 bowl with tomato mixture
toothpicks

Dip meat in olive oil, coating both sides; let the excess oil drip off.
Coat both sides of meat with breadcrumbs.
Place on a clean work area, sprinkle with a little salt and pepper then add a heaping teaspoon of the tomato mixture.
Evenly distribute the tomato mixture leaving a border around the edge of the meat.
Roll up spedini and secure with a couple toothpicks.

Place on prepared baking sheet.
Make sure your oven rack is not directly below the broiler, move it down to the second rung.
Broil for about two minutes on each side; keep your eye on them so they don't burn.

Zucchini Casserole

Serves 6

I didn't create this recipe nor do I know who did. I just remember eating it a lot in the summer at the Farm. I never asked for a recipe, just recreated it from memory… so I don't even know if this is exactly what I ate as a child. What I do know is that it is delicious and I LOVE it! This is a side dish but personally I could eat it as my meal.

Ingredients:

½ c Olive Oil, divided
3 Zucchini, sliced ¼" thick*
¼ c Flour
½ tsp Salt
¼ tsp Pepper
2 Eggs, beaten
2 c Breadcrumbs (pg. 108)
1¼ c Pasta Sauce, divided (pg. 115)
1½ c shredded Mozzarella Cheese, divided
3 T grated Parmigiano-Reggiano, divided

**You can slice your zucchini lengthwise or in rounds, it is totally your choice. It was always in rounds when I was growing up. However, that is a lot more frying so I slice it lengthwise to cut down on time.*

Preheat oven to 325
Spray 8x8 casserole dish with non-stick cooking spray, set aside
In large sauté pan, heat half of the oil over medium-high heat.

Prepare 3 dishes for dredging (pie plates or flat bowls work well):

1. Flour mixed with the salt and pepper
2. Beaten eggs
3. Breadcrumbs

Working in batches, dredge slices of zucchini in flour (shake off excess), then egg (let excess drip off), then breadcrumbs (pack them on).
Put in pan with hot oil and fry until nicely browned, about 3-4 minutes on each side.
Place fried zucchini on a plate lined with a paper towel.
You may need to add some more of the oil between batches; make sure the new oil heats up before you begin with the next batch of frying.

After all the zucchini is fried, start layering your casserole.
Put a ¼ cup of sauce on the bottom of the pan, spread it with a spoon, then layer with:

1. Fried zucchini
2. ¼ cup Sauce
3. ½ cup of the shredded Mozzarella
4. 1 T of Parmesan cheese

Repeat layers 2 more times but on the top layer, spread ½ cup of sauce then proceed with the cheeses.
Put casserole in the oven and bake until brown and bubbly on top, about 25 minutes.
Let rest for 5-10 minutes before serving.

Mangia! Mangia!

Desserts

Biscotti

Black Cake w/ Chocolate Ganache

Blueberry Pie

Cheesecake

Pinwheel Cookies

Snickerdoodles

Spice Cake with Cream Cheese Frosting

Warm Caramel Apple Crisp

Biscotti

About 2 Dozen

Influenced by Aunt May

I had a wonderful day of making several different kinds of cookies with Aunt May and these are my personal favorite to come from that day. To be fair, I changed the ingredients a bit to suit my own tastes. These biscotti are so good I want to have them around all the time. I bake a batch and pop half in the freezer so I can pull them out when I want. Perfect with a cup of coffee or tea... in the morning for breakfast or after dinner for dessert. I love a versatile food, don't you?

Ingredients:

2½ c Flour
1½ tsp Baking Powder
¼ tsp Salt
½ c Butter, softened
1 c Sugar
3 Eggs
1 Vanilla Bean (or 1 T Vanilla Bean Paste)
½ tsp Almond Extract
2 T Grand Marnier
1 c Slivered Almonds

Preheat oven to 375
Line 2 medium baking sheets with parchment paper; set aside.

In a medium bowl, sift together the flour, baking powder and salt; set aside.
In a large mixing bowl, cream the butter and the sugar together using an electric hand mixer.
Add the eggs one at a time, beating thoroughly after each addition.
Scrape the seeds from the vanilla bean and add to mix.
Add almond extract and Grand Marnier; beat until well mixed.

Gradually add the flour mixture to the bowl while continuing to beat, occasionally scraping down the bowl.
Beat just until combined then add the almonds and beat until evenly distributed (the beater will break them up).

Add the dough to a large piping bag (if you don't have one you can substitute a large resealable bag).
Cut the tip off the piping bag so you have a decent size opening (about 1" up from the point).
Pipe dough onto the prepared baking sheets into two equal rectangles about 10" x 5."

Bake for 16-20 minutes until the dough puffs up and turns golden brown.
Remove from oven; let cool for about 15 minutes.
With the long end of the rectangle facing you, use a serrated knife to cut the dough into ½" slices.
Turn the biscotti on their side and put back in the oven; bake for 7 minutes.
Take them out, flip them over and bake for an additional 7 minutes.

As the biscotti cool, they will continue to get crispier to the touch.
They will crunch when you first bite into them but be softer on the inside; absolutely divine!

Black Cake with Chocolate Ganache Serves 8-12
Grandma Scott

Cake is very important to me. I am a cake person through and through. So... when I first met my husband I asked him what his favorite kind of cake was and he responded, "Black Cake." I didn't understand. Black Forest Cake? Chocolate Cake? He held firm at "Black Cake." Eventually, I learned that it is his Grandma Scott's recipe and it WOULD NOT be shared. Once we got married I was allowed to have the recipe. Now my mother-in-law has granted me permission to share it with you. Thank you Karen! The best chocolatey cake ever! I added my own twist by always covering the cake with chocolate ganache instead of traditional chocolate frosting. YUM!

Ingredients:
4 oz Bakers Unsweetened Baking Chocolate
2 c Water, boiling
2 c Sugar
6 T Butter
1 tsp Vanilla
2 c All-Purpose Flour
2 tsp Baking Soda
½ tsp Salt
2 Eggs, lightly beaten

Melt the chocolate in a medium pot.
When completely melted, stir in the 2 cups of boiling water and let boil for 1 minute.
Remove from stove and add the sugar and butter.
Stir until sugar is completely incorporated into the chocolate mixture.
Add vanilla and stir.
Set aside and let cool completely.
**Tip from my mother-in-law: Do this step the night before you want to make the cake. Then you know for sure it is completely cooled.*

Preheat oven to 300
Grease, line with parchment, grease again and flour a 9x3" round cake pan.

When chocolate is cold, in a large mixing bowl sift together the flour, baking soda and salt.
Add eggs and chocolate mixture to the flour.
Mix with an electric hand mixer until the batter is completely blended, occasionally scraping down the sides.
Pour batter into the prepared pan and bake for 75 minutes or until a toothpick comes out clean.

Cool on a rack for 20 minutes then carefully remove the cake from the pan, remove parchment paper and let cool completely. Warning- this is a delicate cake so take extra care or it will break.
Other sizes and cook times:
1. Cupcakes- 18- 20 minutes
2. 9x13" pan- 60 minutes
3. Two 9" Round Cake Pans- Line pans with parchment paper, cook for 30-35 minutes. Cool on wire rack for 20 minutes, carefully remove from pan, remove parchment and cool completely.

Chocolate Ganache

Ingredients:
8 oz semi-sweet Chocolate Chips (about 1 1/3 cups)
¾ c Heavy Cream
1 tsp Vanilla

Optional Ingredients:
1 T Butter (for extra shine)
1 T Brewed Coffee (to enhance the chocolate flavor)
1 tsp Liqueur (such as Grand Marnier)

Heat chocolate chips and cream in a double boiler and stir until smooth.
Add the vanilla at the very end off the heat.
If adding an optional ingredients, add it now then stir all together.
The more you stir, the shinier it will be.

Place the cake (still on the rack) over a rimmed baking sheet lined with parchment paper.
Slowly pour ganache over the cake so it is evenly covered.
You can use the sheet of parchment to "catch" the extra ganache then pour it back into the bowl so it isn't wasted.
*If making cupcakes, just turn them upside down and dip them into the bowl of ganache, done!

Blueberry Pie

Serves 8

We started "Summer Desserts" a few years ago. We create a list of desserts I have never baked from scratch and we make our way down the list throughout the summer. I bake; we all eat. It's a fun tradition for our family and a great way for me to learn new skills. Blueberry Pie was my husband's choice that first summer in 2014. Now he tries to choose it every summer, but that is against the rules.

Ingredients:
2 Pie Crusts
5 c Blueberries
Zest of ½ of 1 Lemon
1 T fresh Lemon Juice
½ c Sugar
¼ c Flour
¼ tsp Cinnamon
¼ tsp Salt
1½ T Butter, cut into small pieces

Make sure the oven rack is in the lower 1/3 of the oven then preheat it to 425.

Combine the blueberries, lemon zest, lemon juice, sugar, flour, cinnamon and salt in a bowl. Gently stir together and let sit for 15 minutes

Use one pie crust to line the bottom of your pie plate.
Pour in fruit mixture.
Dot the butter all over the top of the blueberries.
Top with 2nd pie crust and seal the edges.
**I like to make a lattice top. If you put on the whole crust on top, cut vents so the steam can escape.*

Bake for 30 minutes.
Reduce the oven to 350 and bake for an additional 25-35 minutes or until the bottom crust has cooked and the top crust is a dark golden brown.
**I always use a pie shield for the edges so they don't burn.*

Cheesecake

Serves A Crowd

Aunt Joy

This cheesecake is amazing! Even people who don't care for cheesecake LOVE this cheesecake. Yes, it takes a long time and is a lot of work but it is 100% worth the effort. I always make the cheesecake a day in advance and decorate the top the day of the party. It's nice to have a make-ahead showstopper! Another bonus, it serves a ton of people. I have never seen this cheesecake finished in one setting… which is great because I can always snack on it later!

Cookie Crust Ingredients:
2 c Flour
½ c Sugar
12 T Butter, softened
2 Egg Yolks, slightly beaten
1 tsp Vanilla Extract

Sift flour and sugar into a medium bowl.
Cut in the butter with a pastry blender until mixture is crumbly.
Add 2 slightly beaten egg yolks and vanilla.
Mix lightly with fork just until pastry holds together and leaves side of bowl.
Chill the dough in the fridge for about 15 minutes.

Preheat oven to 400
Pat 1/3 of the chilled cookie dough evenly over bottom of a 10-inch spring form pan.
Bake for 8 minutes, or till lightly brown.
When cool enough to handle, pat remaining dough evenly onto sides of pan to make a shell.
Chill.

Cheesecake Filling Ingredients:
5- 8oz bricks Cream Cheese, softened
1¾ c Sugar
3 T Flour
1 tsp Vanilla Extract
5 Eggs
2 Egg Yolks
1 pint Sour Cream

Preheat oven to 450
Beat cream cheese, sugar, flour and vanilla in a large bowl with an electric mixer at medium speed till smooth and fluffy.
Beat in eggs and yolks one at a time; stir in sour cream.
Pour mixture into a spring form pan with baked bottom crust and unbaked shell.
Bake at 450 for 12 minutes.

Lower oven to 250 and bake for 1½ hours.
Turn off oven and let cake remain in the oven for 1 hour.
Remove from oven and cool completely.
Store the cheesecake in the refrigerator until ready to serve; take out of pan before you refrigerate.
Serve plain or with your favorite topping… I love fresh berries and a drizzle of ganache.

Pinwheel Cookies

3 Dozen Cookies

Aunt May

Pinwheel cookies are just so much fun! They are cute, dainty little two-bite cookies that are great for dessert, served with tea and they look fabulous on a holiday cookie platter. These cookies also freeze beautifully! Slice them up, freeze them for 20 minutes uncovered, then put them in a freezer bag. You can bake them off whenever you feel like having a little treat.

Ingredients:

2 c Flour (plus extra for sprinkling)
2 tsp Baking Powder
½ tsp Salt
½ c Butter, softened
¾ c Sugar
½ c Brown Sugar, firmly packed
1 Egg
1 tsp Vanilla Extract
2 T Cocoa Powder

In a medium bowl, sift together the flour, baking powder and salt. Set aside.
In a large mixing bowl, cream the butter, sugar and brown sugar.
Add the egg and vanilla extract.
Continue to beat while gradually adding the flour mixture; occasionally scraping down the sides of the bowl with a spatula.
Do as much as you can with the electric mixer then use a spatula to finish combining.

Divide the batter into 2 equal portions.
Add cocoa powder to one of the portions of dough and mix completely.
Wrap each portion of dough in plastic wrap and refrigerate for 20 minutes.

On a piece of wax paper, roll out the vanilla dough into a rectangle about 9"x12" and 1/8" thick.
Repeat with the chocolate dough, trying to get the same size rectangle.
Flip the chocolate cookie dough on top of the vanilla cookie dough.
Roll very lightly with the rolling pin once or twice (just to press the two doughs together a bit, not to make bigger).

Have the short end of the rectangle closest to you; trim both short ends so they each have a clean line.
Cut the dough in half lengthwise to form two 6"x9" rectangles; now the "long" end of each rectangle is closest to you.
With the long end in front of you, start to roll up the cookies as tightly as you can; use the wax paper to help you roll.
Roll each log in a piece of wax paper; twist one end of the wax paper and hold.

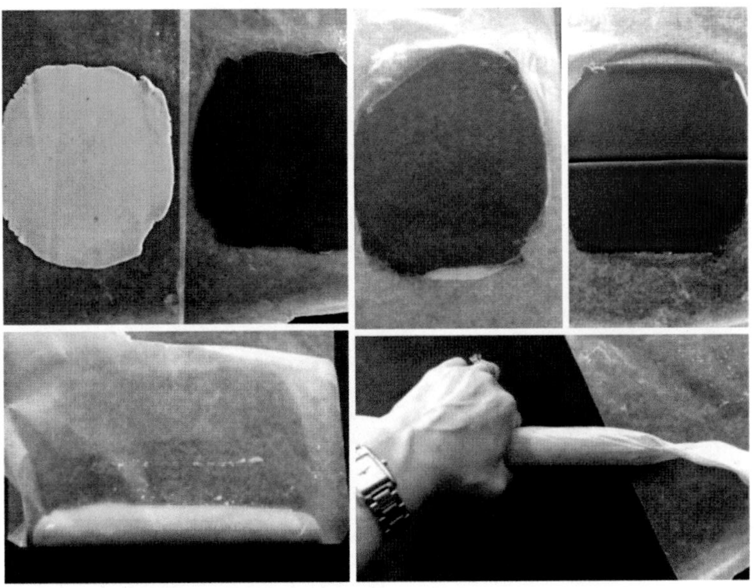

Using the thumb and pointer finger of your other hand, form a circle.
Squeeze down the length of the cookie roll a few times: this will squeeze the two types of dough together and make sure all your cookies are equal in diameter.
Repeat this process with the other log.
Refrigerate each log for a minimum of 30 minutes.

Preheat oven to 400

Line cookie sheet(s) with parchment paper.
Remove dough from parchment roll and slice cookies evenly, about ¼" thick.
Bake until just lightly golden in color, about 8-10 minutes.

Snickerdoodles

Makes 5 Dozen

Aunt Clare (from her mom)

I think Snickerdoodles are my favorite cookies. Aunt Clare used her mom's recipe but added baking the cookies on a parchment lined baking sheet to prevent the bottoms from burning. I changed the order of chilling. I find my cookies attain that perfect soft snickerdoodle consistency if I chill the dough right before throwing them in the oven. You can also place the rolled, cinnamon/sugar coated dough balls on a baking sheet, freeze them for 30 minutes then put them in a freezer bag. Store them in the freezer and they will always be on hand. You can bake off as many or as few as you want, whenever you want. Genius!

Ingredients:

2¾ c Flour
2 tsp Cream of Tartar
1 tsp Baking Soda
½ tsp Salt
1 c soft Shortening
1½ c Sugar
2 Eggs
2 T Sugar
2 tsp Cinnamon

In a medium bowl, sift together flour, cream of tartar, baking soda and salt.
In a large mixing bowl, cream shortening and sugar with and electric mixer.
Add eggs and beat until well combined.
Add dry ingredients and blend w/ electric mixer as long as you can, then switch to a spatula if you need to.
Using clean hands, roll the dough into balls the size of small walnuts.

In a small bowl, combine 2 tablespoons of sugar and 2 teaspoons of cinnamon.
Roll each ball into the cinnamon/sugar mixture.
Place about 2 inches apart on a parchment lined baking sheet.
When baking sheet is full, place in the fridge for 30 minutes or in the freezer for 10 minutes.

Preheat oven to 400

After chilling, put cookies into the oven and bake for 8-10 minutes, until cookies spread and crack but are still soft.

Spice Cake with Cream Cheese Frosting

Serves 8-12

Spice cake is one of my Dad's favorite kinds of cake. The only one I ever made from scratch was ok but not any better than a box mix. Since I couldn't find a "from scratch" recipe I liked, I set out to create my own delicious recipe. I am happy to say this one is a winner!

Cake Ingredients:
2 c Flour
1 tsp Baking Powder
1 tsp Baking Soda
½ tsp Kosher Salt
2 tsp Cinnamon
1 tsp Nutmeg
½ tsp Ginger
½ tsp Allspice
½ tsp Ground Cloves
1 c Vegetable Oil
1 c Brown Sugar
1 c White Sugar
4 Eggs (at room temperature)
1 c Buttermilk

Preheat the oven to 325
Grease and flour two 9" round cake pans.

In a medium bowl, sift together the first 9 ingredients.
In a large mixing bowl, beat the oil, brown sugar and white sugar with an electric mixer until well blended.
Beat the eggs in one at a time.
Alternately mix in the buttermilk and dry ingredients, beginning and ending with the buttermilk.

Divide the batter evenly between the two cake pans; tap the pans on the counter a few times to get the bubbles out.
Bake for 35-40 minutes or until a toothpick comes out clean.

Cool in the pan on a rack for 10 minutes; remove from pan and cool on the rack completely.

Frosting Ingredients:
12 oz Cream Cheese, softened
6 T Unsalted Butter, at room temperature
1½ tsp Vanilla Extract
2¼ c Powdered Sugar

Using an electric mixer, beat the cream cheese and butter together.
Beat in the vanilla extract.
Beat in the powdered sugar until everything is well combined.

To Frost The Cake

You can make a 2-layer cake and just frost as usual. But a 4-layer cake is very pretty.

If desired, use a cake knife to cut each cake layer in half horizontally so you end up with 4 equal layers of cake.
Divide the icing in the bowl into 4 equal portions; this is just so you have uniform layers of cake and icing.
Place one layer of cake on your serving plate.
Ice only the top of the cake with one portion of icing.
Put the next cake layer on top and ice only the top of that layer, and so on and so forth
I leave the sides naked for a "rustic" look.

If you want to decorate, you can sprinkle some cinnamon or top with some pieces of candied ginger.

If decorating for the holidays, you can cut a shape (snowflake, snowman, star, etc.) out of a piece of parchment paper, gently lay on top of the cake and sprinkle cinnamon inside the "stencil."

Warm Caramel Apple Crisp

Serves 8-12

I am not a pie person. I don't like soft syrupy fruit. But, for some reason, I can't get enough of this caramel apple crisp. It is a great dessert for any occasion but I really love it as the finale of a holiday meal. You can prepare the dessert ahead of time and keep it in the fridge. Throw it in the oven when you are sitting down to dinner and it will be ready right in time for dessert. Delicious served with vanilla ice cream and champagne!

Ingredients:
6 Honey Crisp Apples (Fuji & Granny Smith also work well or a combo of all three)
1 T fresh Lemon Juice
¼ c Sugar
1 T Flour
½ tsp Cinnamon
1 jar Caramel Sauce, divided

Crumble Topping:
¾ c Flour
½ c Brown Sugar
½ c Oats
½ tsp Salt
½ c Cold Butter, cut into small pieces

Preheat oven to 350
Spray an 8x8 glass pan with non-stick cooking spray.
Peel apples and cut large chunks of flesh off, leaving only the core.
Then, slice each apple chunk into thin slices.
In medium bowl, toss the apple slices with lemon juice.

Add sugar, flour, and cinnamon, toss all together.
Pour in ¼ cup of the caramel sauce and mix until evenly coated.
Spread apples into prepared dish.

Combine first 4 ingredients for the crumble topping in a medium bowl.
Add the butter and cut into the oat mixture using a pastry blender or two butter knives until the butter is the size of small peas.
Spread the crumble topping evenly over the apples.
Drizzle a few more tablespoons of caramel sauce over the top of the crumble.

Bake for 45 minutes until the apples bubble and the topping is golden brown.

Menu Options

Brunch Buffet
Egg Casserole...17
Orange Fruit Salad...19
Overnight French Toast...20
Banana Bread...26
Hashbrown Casserole...74
Baked Ham...85
Cheesecake...131

Tea Party/Shower
Egg Salad Sandwiches...17
Quiche...22
Smoked Salmon Spread...24
Maple Bacon Scones...28
Creamy Broiled Tomatoes...71
Boiled Teeny Tiny Potatoes...81
Pinwheel Cookies...132
Victoria Sandwich (Blog)

Cocktail Party
7 Layer Greek Dip...60
Boursin Ball...61
Deviled Eggs...62
Veal Spinach Loaf...67
Mini Spedini...124
Spice Cake Cupcakes with Cream Cheese Frosting...135
Candied Pecans (Blog)

Football Party
Chili...36
Giant Rare Roast Beef Sandwich...54
Guacamole...64
Buffalo Chicken Dip (Blog)
Brookies (Blog)

Greek Feast
Cucumber & Tomato Salad...43
Roasted Asparagus...77
Roasted Teeny Tiny Potatoes...81
Brian's Lamb Lollipops...91
Vanilla Ice Cream with Salted Caramel Sauce (Blog)

Italian Night
Mom's Salad...44
Stuffed Artichokes...66
Pork Ragu...116
Spedini...124
Ricotta Orange Pound Cake (Blog)

Steak Dinner
Caesar Salad...42
Creamed Spinach...70
Potatoes on the Grill...79
The Perfect Steak...104
Black Cake with Chocolate Ganache...128

Spring
Strawberry Spinach Salad...47
Herbed Veggies...79
Lemon Chicken on the Grill...94
Angel Food Trifle (Blog)

Summer
Barbecued Chicken...86
Potato Salad...76
Baked Beans...69
Corn on the Cobb...79
Cucumber & Tomato Salad...43
Blueberry Pie,,,130

Fall
Gravy...73
Roasted Carrots...77
Sautéed Mushrooms...78
Mashed Potatoes (Blog)
Roasted Pork Loin...98
Warm Apple Crisp...137

Winter
Grandma's Green Beans & Potatoes...72
Oven Roasted Brisket...95
Hawaiian Rolls (Store Bought)
Sticky Toffee Pudding (Blog)

Acknowledgements

There is no possible way I can accurately express my gratitude to all those who have made this book possible. There are so many of you who have been on this journey with me over the last four years.

Obvious thanks are in order to all my family and friends who so generously shared their recipes. Thank you for letting me use your recipes and contact you multiple times while trying to get them just right. Thank you for letting me come to your house and cook with you. Thank you for letting me take your picture (even though most of you did NOT want your picture taken) and list your names in the book. It was very important to me that you get the recognition you deserve.

There is so much more to a cookbook than just gathering recipes, which is why there are so many others I have to thank. Thank you to all my cousins and friends (especially Ellie, Stacey, Amie, Lisa and Jami) for letting me bring plates of food to your house even though you didn't want me to, for being my guinea pigs and for testing my recipes in your own kitchens. Thank you Anne, Stephanie and Meribeth for the constant support and encouragement. Thank you all for your feedback and input when I couldn't make decisions.

Thank you to my brother for having the most positive attitude of anyone in the entire world and for trying to will it on me (no matter how much I resist). Your optimism is both inspiring and encouraging.

To my father, thank you for being a man who loves being in the kitchen. You were the one who made food a centerpiece of our lives. It is by your example that I learned of the passion and joy that comes from creating a meal and sharing it with loved ones.

To my daughters, you are everything to me. You will never be able to fully understand how fierce my love for you is, but know it is unwavering and eternal. Thank you for being the wonderful young ladies you are (and excellent little food critics).

Thank you to my wonderful husband for putting up with everything! Thank you for providing for our family, which allowed me to pursue my dream. Thank you for pushing me when I needed to be pushed. You continue to give me everything I ever wished for as a little girl. I love you.

To my mother and my sister for being there every single step of the way. You are my sounding boards, my support system, my therapists, my biggest cheerleaders and even my editors. I truly could not have done this without you. It is true that I needed everyone but I needed you two the most. It is not possible to articulate how much you have done for me, how grateful I am or how much I love you, but I hope you know.

Recipe Index

Breakfast & Brunch

Breads

Soups

Salads

Sandwiches

Appetizers

Sides

Main Courses

Italian

Desserts

Made in the USA
Monee, IL
21 July 2022

10111403R00086